Edited by Esmeralda Santiago
and Joie Davidow

Las Mamis

Esmeralda Santiago is the author of the memoirs *When I Was Puerto Rican* and *Almost a Woman*, and of the novel *América's Dream*. She lives in Westchester County, New York.

Joie Davidow founded *L.A. Style*, *L.A. Weekly*, and *Sí*, a national Latino lifestyle publication. The author of *Infusions of Healing: A Treasury of Mexican-American Herbal Remedies*, she lives in Los Angeles.

Together they are the editors of the anthology *Las Christmas*, available in English and Spanish from Vintage. Esmeralda Santiago's *When I Was Puerto Rican* and *Almost a Woman* are also available in English and Spanish from Vintage.

Also edited by Esmeralda Santiago and Joie Davidow

Las Christmas

Also by Esmeralda Santiago

Almost a Woman

América's Dream

When I Was Puerto Rican

Also by Joie Davidow

Infusions of Healing: A Treasury of
Mexican-American Herbal Remedies

Las Mamis

Las Mamis

Favorite Latino Authors
Remember Their Mothers

Edited by

ESMERALDA SANTIAGO and JOIE DAVIDOW

VINTAGE BOOKS

A Division of Random House, Inc.

New York

FIRST VINTAGE BOOKS EDITION, MAY 2001

Copyright © 2000 by Esmeralda Santiago and Joie Davidow

The photograph that accompanies Alba Ambert's essay is courtesy of Antonio Sánchez
Gaetán, Universidad del Sagrado Corazón, Puerto Rico.

The Library of Congress has catalogued the Knopf edition as follows:

Las mamis : favorite authors remember their mothers / Esmeralda Santiago and Joie

Davidow, editors.

ix, 189 p. : 23 cm.

ISBN: 0-375-40879-7

1. Hispanic American women—Biography—Anecdotes. 2. Mothers—United States—

Biography—Anecdotes. 3. Hispanic American families—Anecdotes.

E184.S75 M365 2000

306.874/3/08968073 21

Vintage ISBN: 0-375-72687-X

Author photo © Rudi Weislein

www.vintagebooks.com

Printed in the United States of America
10 9 8 7 6 5 4 3 2 1

Contents

Florence Schwartz, Joie's mother,
just before she got married (1940s)

Foreword

The first great passion in life is for the woman whose body we once shared. Her breath was our breath; her blood coursed through our veins; her heart set the rhythm for the beat of our own. The connection between mother and child is the most essential bond possible for each of us. But the relationship can take infinite forms, influenced by circumstance, culture, and religion.

Through my work as editor of *Sí* magazine, and later as co-editor of our previous anthology, *Las Christmas*, I began to realize that Latina mothers have a particular role in the lives of their children. These women—many of them immigrants with little or no English, and with no resources other than their own inner strength—have often managed to raise children of great achievement against great odds. And rich or poor, they link their children to something precious that might be otherwise lost: to another country, another time, another language—the mother tongue. This anthology, then, is a celebration of the often endearing, sometimes maddening women who have formed a generation of Latinos with their great courage, strength, and love.

As Esmeralda and I began to work on *Las Mamis*, my own mother died. I knew that every mother has to die sometime, and Mommy was lucky enough to have lived a long life and to die in her own bed, after suffering through only one awful night. But I felt as bereft as if the love of my life had forsaken me. So it was with a certain sense of irony that in those first sorrowful months following my mother's death I found myself talking with writers about the relationship I had so recently lost.

We were surprised that so many writers declined our invitation. One writer told me frankly that it wasn't worth the risk of invoking his mami's displeasure. For others, the relationship was too wounded to be laid bare on a page without spilling blood and tears, or so fragile that any attempt to capture it in a web of words, however delicately constructed, might shatter it. A few writers gladly accepted, only to become paralyzed when they realized what they were about to do. Writing something about Mami that she would actually *read* terrified a couple of them into backing out at the last minute. Even the most facile among us suffered and struggled and begged for more time. One contributor told me that he wondered what "devices" the others had used, as though Mami's reaction was a daunting obstacle that had to be negotiated around. No matter what we call them—Mom, Mommy, Mamá, Mami, or Mamacita—our mothers have enormous power over us all.

Many of the authors who accepted our challenge stunned us with their courageous honesty. I felt a little jealous of those whose mothers were still living, no matter how difficult the relationship might be. I wanted to urge them to make the most of her, to visit her, to tell her anything that was in their hearts, even though she might be unable to hear them. In some of the most moving essays, we sensed that the author used our book as a way of making amends with Mami, of showing her that she was appreciated after all. And many of the authors were able to begin to understand Mami's point of view, to demystify the mother and see her as a woman, not as a powerful being who had given or not given, but as a fellow adult, who had struggled and tried and sometimes failed.

The anthology came together while I grieved for my own mommy. In the acuteness of sorrow, as I read the memoirs of all the sons and daughters who contributed to this book, I understood why writing about Mami was so hard. I saw that all of us live, not standing alone, a solitary tree in the wilderness, but in the shadow of the older tree that begot us. No matter how we struggle to be wholly separate, no matter how far away we plant ourselves, we are destined to exist in relation to our mothers, to the very source of our lives. Our achievements are their achievements. Our failures are their failures. Our dreams are only variations of those our mothers dreamed for us. We reject their expectations, or strive to live up to them, but we live our lives forever in the shadow of theirs.

Joie Davidow

Las Mamis

Ramona Santiago, Esmeralda Santiago's mother

"We constantly complain to one another about her eccentricities and startling prejudices, just as we take for granted her generosity, capacity for love, and ability to overlook her children's shortcomings while she criticizes the same behavior in others."

ᖇ ᖇ ᖇ ᖇ ᖇ ᖇ ESMERALDA SANTIAGO

Esmeralda Santiago is the author of the memoirs When I Was Puerto Rican *and* Almost a Woman, *and of the novel* América's Dream. *She is also coeditor, with Joie Davidow, of* Las Christmas: Favorite Latino Authors Share Their Holiday Memories. *She is a graduate of Harvard University, and holds a Master of Fine Arts degree from Sarah Lawrence College.*

First Born

I was her first child, born feetfirst, the umbilical cord snug around my neck. My father's mother delivered her of me. I fell into Abuela's hands, a blue baby, and Mami thought I was dead. Abuela slapped me hard, and when I wailed, she returned me to my mother's body, to the full, soft warmth of her breast. Maybe it was that perilous beginning that bound me to her at the moment when she sent me forth. Since that rainy Monday morning, whenever I'm breathless and abused, I return to her bosom, hungry.

She was sixteen when I was conceived. My father was twenty-eight and already had a child with another woman. I've never asked her how they met, how he seduced her, how she managed to evade her mother and brother and the house full of aunts and uncles with whom she lived so she could be with him. Whenever I ask personal questions, she says she doesn't remember, but a few days later she'll volunteer what she wants me to know. That's how I found out that, around the time they met, she worked as a clerk in her uncle's pastry shop in Santurce. Was it there that Papi first saw her, dark-eyed, fresh-faced, eager for adventure?

It was August when they made me, the middle of hurricane season. I imagine a hot, dry day. Or had the sky rumbled and cracked in one of those unexpectedly violent summer storms that break over Puerto Rico with no warning? She's afraid of lightning and thunder. Perhaps he held her in his arms to calm the trembling that accompanies her fears.

I was a fussy, sleepless infant, dark and hairy, given to fits of rage that ended as suddenly and inexplicably as they began. I slept in a hammock that Mami swung rhythmically in an attempt to soothe the colic, heat rash, mosquito bites: the irritants I couldn't name but that made her life miserable. Years later she'd wish for my children to give me as much trouble as I had given her, and the possibility kept me childless into my thirties.

Before I was two, I had a baby sister. We lived in a one-room house on stilts over muddy water. Wobbly planks led to the street. When we walked across them, Mami clutched my hand and held Delsa against her bosom.

"Don't let go," she warned. "Be careful, or you'll fall and drown." As we reached the street, her grip eased and my fears melted, to be renewed again on the way back over the long, splintery boards that creaked and groaned with every step.

"But you can't possibly remember that," Mami challenges,

and I ask, did we live in a house over muddy water? Were there planks leading to the road? She admits that yes, both things are true, but refuses to believe I can remember that far back. "I must have told you about it when you were older," she claims.

On a sleepy afternoon, Mami and I sat at a table near a window, listening to the water slap against the pilings that held up the house. I sucked my thumb while, with my other hand inside my panties, I bothered the place where pee came from. When she saw what I was doing, Mami flew off her chair, grabbed my arm, and spanked me, screaming that I was never to do that, it was dirty, girls shouldn't touch themselves down there.

That's the first beating I remember, the sting of her hand against my buttocks, the strong fist around my wrist, the flat sound of her fingers against my skin.

She was not the only mother to hit her children. *Una pela* was a common threat by parents then—still is—and it was not unusual for parents to peel skin off with a nubby guava switch or with a stiff leather belt. Papi used his belt on us. Mami used her hands, a rope, a shoe, a frying pan, whatever was closest.

In spite of the many *pelas* I endured, I don't think of myself as a battered child. That term didn't enter my vocabulary until I was in my twenties and newspapers and television broadcasts were filled with stories of children burned with lit cigarettes, tied up to bedsteads, clubbed with broomsticks, locked up in closets, left to starve. I remembered my mother's rage, her violence, and was ashamed that she'd ever raised her hand to me and my siblings. I couldn't excuse it, but I forgave it. I forced myself to look beyond resentment to who she was when she, and we, were growing up. And in looking at her life I found lessons. Chief among them: don't dwell in the past or you will drown in sorrow.

⌒ ⌒ ⌒

Norma was born when I was four, and while she was still a toddler we moved to Macún, a barrio in the municipality of Toa Baja, where Papi owned a *parcela*, a plot of land which boasted eleven avocado and five mango trees, pigeon pea and annatto bushes, wild oregano, and a spiny lemon tree. The ramshackle house on the *parcela* had no electricity or running water. Barrels under the corner eaves collected rain. There was a pond down the road, the scummy, green surface broken by bubbles that Mami imagined were the breath of creatures in its depths. Pregnant with her fourth child, Mami stayed home while Papi spent most of the week building or renovating houses in San Juan.

In the last weeks of her pregnancy, the barrels were empty and the sky cloudless. Delsa, Norma, and I whimpered from hunger, but there was no water to cook the rice. The louder we cried the more desperate Mami became, until finally, she walked to the pond and drew a bucket of water.

"I strained it through cotton, then let the water boil a long time." Her face twisted into disgust as she told me the story years later. "The white rice still came out green. I sobbed as we ate it. I figured if it was poisonous, we would at least die together." As she spoke, I was filled with compassion for her as she was then, twenty-one years old, with three toddlers and another baby on the way, a city girl stranded in the wilderness of a barrio in *el campo*, alone.

After my brother, Héctor, was born, Mami and Papi seemed to fight more. She accused, he defended himself. She cried, he sulked. She told him to leave her alone, he disappeared, to return days later as if nothing had happened. My sisters and brother and I cowered in our hammocks, or stayed clear of them when Papi was home. We watched her face for signs that a fight was coming, listened to her tone of voice and whether she set the pots down gently or banged them upon the cooking stones. If she was in a dark mood, we were silent and watchful, sub-servient to her whims.

When they were getting along, they worked at opposite ends of the *parcela*. As she collected *gandules* for dinner, he built stur-dier walls. His hammer kept time to the Mexican *rancheras* he sang in a clear baritone, she moved her hips back and forth as she hummed boleros and dropped the fat pigeon pea pods into a metal bowl. I've always thought that words belonged to him, but music has always been hers—the wordless hum of effort re-warded.

With four young children to take care of, Mami had little time for socializing. But when the public water fountain was installed about a mile from our house, she met some of the neighbor women. Several times a week, we walked over to col-lect fresh water. While Mami and the *vecinas* stood around the fountain filling their buckets and jabbering, we stomped on the mud from the spillover. From time to time, one of them looked in our direction and yelled at us to stop. But as soon as she turned around, we went back to smearing ourselves, and each other, with mud.

After her visit with the neighbors, Mami filled two large pails, then carried them down the dirt road, her arms straining. We trailed her, each with our own can filled to the brim, arguing about who would spill the least on the way back. Once home, she stored the water in huge square lard cans topped with a wooden cover. This was our drinking, cooking, and teeth-brushing water, boiled daily before use. For washing, she still poured buckets of rainwater into the tin tubs.

Sometimes I still catch Mami scrubbing a blouse by hand in the bathroom sink, her fingers fisted around the garment, her knuckles rubbing the fabric in even, confident strokes, as sudsy bubbles drip down her wrists to her elbows. There's a slight smile on her face, and stern concentration—the triumph of will and strength over dirt.

While I didn't understand it then, it now appears inevitable that Mami would want to return to the city. Life in Macún was hard; and with my father gone most of the time, and in spite of the visits with the *vecinas* by the public fountain, she was lonesome. One day she picked us up from school and moved us to Santurce, closer to those of her aunts and uncles who had not fled to the United States in search of work. They dropped in on Sunday afternoons to share the letters received from their siblings in New York and to gossip about them over endless cups of sweetened *café con leche*.

In Santurce Mami smiled more. She knew how to handle herself in the city, liked the convenience of a couple of blocks to the store instead of a couple of miles to the cooperative that might or might not have what she needed. On lazy evenings, we walked around the plaza, where she bought shaved ice in paper cones with sweet jewel-bright syrup poured over it. Sometimes we caught a bus at the corner near our house and got off in front of her uncle's pastry shop, where we chose a *tembleque* or a square of coconut rice. While she talked with her aunt and uncle, we played with our cousins in the porch, every so often returning to stare hungrily at the cool glass cases filled with more sweets than we'd ever seen in one place.

Mami was in her early twenties then, and, in spite of four pregnancies in less than six years, she looked good and enjoyed dressing up. Instead of the cotton shifts and bare feet of Macún, she now wore stiff starched and ironed blouses and skirts, high-heel shoes, hair curled or twisted into a bun at the nape of her neck. She wore rouge and lipstick, too, and powder on her nose.

She constantly told us to speak softer, to stop running, to sit still, to keep our clothes clean, and to wash our feet and scrub under our fingernails.

Papi came to see us, and eventually to stay with us. Soon after Alicia was born, he convinced Mami to return to Macún, and we did, with city manners and clothes ill-suited to the country. The *vecinas* criticized her for acting as if we were better than everyone else in the barrio just because we'd lived in Santurce. At the water fountain, they looked away when we approached carrying our vessels, no better nor worse than theirs.

It still hurts me to recall how hard it was for Mami after we returned. The look on her face as we approached the water fountain was a lesson in quiet dignity. Her lips tight, her lively eyes focused on one of us or on the task at hand, she asserted her *dignidad* as the neighbors turned their backs on her or made comments that she was sure to hear but pretended not to. It took weeks to win them over again, as if we had to prove we would stay this time before they could trust us.

Like most of the women in Macún, Mami made all our clothes on a black Singer treadle sewing machine. She also cut and hand-stitched the cotton diapers and baby blankets of which there never seemed to be enough. For everyday wear she made me and my sisters sleeveless cotton shifts out of fabrics stamped with tiny flowers and vines. For special occasions, she sewed dresses with rows of lacy ruffles, itchy cancans and long sashes that tied into bows at the back.

She liked to dress us alike, and tried her best to make us look like triplets, even though we were all different sizes and skin tones. I was brown, skinny, taller than Delsa or Norma. Delsa was darker, petite, with slanted onyx eyes and wavy black hair that Mami shaped with her fingers into corkscrews around her head. Mami called Norma "*la colorá*" because of her rosy skin and curly hair that framed her narrow face in fuzzy red-brown ringlets.

Unlike my sisters', my hair was too straight to stay in any of the shapes Mami tried to impose on it. Sometimes she cut squares of paper that she folded around locks of wet hair before I went to bed. When she took them off the next morning, the limp spirals lasted just long enough for her to see the potential.

One day, she washed my hair, trimmed it, then dabbed on a liquid that she swore would curl my hair. It smelled like burning rubber mixed with lemon juice, and it tingled my scalp as she put it on. She rolled strands of hair tightly around pink plastic bones. She then had me sit in the sun for the time it took my shadow to crawl from my right side to my left. "The permanent has to set," she said.

When she unrolled the bones, my scalp felt as if it had separated from my skull, and my hair smelled burnt. She handed me Papi's shaving mirror, where I saw a black, frizzy halo around a scowling face. "You look like a startled monkey," she laughed.

Every time a feast day or other special occasion approached, she came home from the cooperative market with a new permanent kit. I hid behind the oregano or annatto bushes, but she called me back with threats that I was afraid to ignore. After many attempts (to this day she says she only did it once), she agreed that my hair was never going to be like Delsa's, Norma's, or baby Alicia's, so she stopped trying. I have an aversion to hair salons and treatments that I trace to those hot afternoons in our yard while the smelly permanent solution set and Mami promised Shirley Temple curls if I just sat in the sun a little longer.

~ ~ ~

Edna was born in Macún, into a house that was beginning to have some of the conveniences we'd taken for granted in Santurce. Electricity buzzed along thick wires strung from pole to pole into the funnel end of the barrio. The single bulb that Papi dangled from the ceiling of our house dispersed a sharp white light that dimmed and brightened or went out altogether, depending on the path of the wind. The nights now seemed blacker than when we'd lit them with kerosene lamps. Creatures that had stayed outside before, now flew or crawled in, as if they, too, were afraid of the dark. The mysterious corners of the house that the flicker of the *quinqués* didn't reach were now visible. We could no longer pretend that the bunch of bananas hanging from the rafters was an enormous bat, or that the bundles of clothes against the walls were pirates in hiding.

When we used kerosene lamps, we went to bed "*con las gallinas.*" Soon as the hens went up to roost, Mami gathered us to bathe and brush our teeth and cuddle into our hammocks or narrow cots. But electricity made the days longer. We could now stay up playing while Mami mended. When he was home, Papi built shelves along the walls, or added a counter to the kitchen. During the day, we spent most of our time outdoors, but with electric light, the interior of the house took on new importance. It was during our newly short nights that Mami began to dream of curtains for the windows, and a proper living-room set with a sofa and chairs and a coffee table. Little by little, these items appeared in our house, the furniture delivered on a rickety truck that pulled up to the hard dirt of our front yard in gusts of black smoke and the excitement of squealing metal.

I suspect that it was the modernization of Macún that drove Mami out of there. As electricity and plumbing made their way into the barrio, she was more aware of how neither of these things were novelties in Santurce. And in New York, where her mother and most of her relatives lived, Mami said they laughed to hear our neighbors boast of no longer having to draw water from a barrel in order to take a bath in the same tub used for the laundry.

We left Macún soon after Raymond was born. This time, Papi came with us, although their arguments, which they called *discusiones* but we called fights, didn't abate. The reason they were called *discusiones* is that they were never physically violent. Rather, their battles were waged with words, except for the occasional object thrown by one or the other, which always managed to miss its target. After their more acrimonious *discusiones*, Mami moved us, as if the biggest statement she could make to Papi was that no matter what he did or said, we children belonged to her.

When Raymond was four, Mami took him to New York to seek medical attention for his foot, which had been injured in a bicycle accident. She returned to Puerto Rico asking us to go to the "*bodega*" for "*un contéiner de leche,*" instead of a bottle of milk, or "*pan de eslái,*" bread already sliced in neat squares, rather than the long, crusty loaves we'd always eaten.

In my thirteenth year, just before her thirtieth birthday, she took me, Edna, and Raymond to New York, leaving the rest of my siblings with Papi until she could send for them. She was convinced that life in New York would be easier, better, more comfortable. She talked about how great an education we would all receive, how many opportunities there were for a woman skilled in the use of a sewing machine and willing to work hard.

Did she notice, during the month she spent with her mother before she brought us over, that Tata drank beer or wine every day until she couldn't stand up? Did she see that the apartments where Tata lived were run-down, that graffiti was scrawled on building walls, that garbage cans were tied with chains to the lampposts or rattled against low wrought-iron fences? Had she heard that in the United States people spoke a different language than they did in Puerto Rico? Did anyone tell her about winter?

I remember that a few weeks after we moved to Brooklyn, I took a quiz in the Spanish newspaper—"Are You an Optimist, or a Pessimist?"—and the results showed that Mami was one and I was the other.

This is what Mami saw in Brooklyn: Our high-ceilinged brick-and-mortar apartments were solid and impervious to hurricanes. We had indoor plumbing. The electricity never failed if we kept up with the payments. In the bodega across the street we could find whatever we needed. In Manhattan's garment district there were plenty of jobs.

This is what I saw: We were cooped up day and night to keep us from the crime and violence of the street. There was one bathroom for nine people, and whatever you did inside it was heard and smelled by anyone waiting outside. Electricity meant there was never any silence, because our hours were filled with the blare of Top 40 radio and television game shows. The mango I was able to pick off the tree in Puerto Rico now cost more than train fare to Manhattan. Mami worked long hours making bras, for which she was paid by the piece, so that she never knew exactly how much money she'd bring home the next payday. Sometimes she'd arrive at work on a Monday and the bra factory would have closed over the weekend, and no one could tell her how to claim the money she'd earned for the previous two weeks' work. When she didn't have enough money, we had to go to the welfare office, where American people who spoke no Spanish did their best to humiliate us before grudgingly agreeing to help.

Her belief that things would turn out fine moderated my certainty that whatever could go wrong, would. But Mami was not deterred by my pessimism. She trudged forward, willed us to accompany her on what would prove to be our life's adventure. A different environment, culture, language, and history did not faze her. Rather, the changes energized her, fired her into pushing herself, and us, far beyond the limits we set for ourselves.

"What do you mean, you can't learn English?" she argued when one of us was frustrated with the language. "I'm not as young as you are, but I dare to kick English around when necessary."

What she referred to as "*mi inglés to' estropea'o*" became good enough so that she could manage when we weren't there to interpret. Her bruised English got her through late-night visits to the emergency rooms of hospitals with Francisco, the man she fell in love with a few months after we arrived in the United States. It helped her exchange a few words with the nurses who brought her news of how Francisco's cancer surgery and postoperative therapy were going. It came in handy at the Social Security Administration when she had to claim survivor benefits for their son, Franky, who was born a few months before his father died. It was useful when she rented one apartment after another, in search of the perfect place for herself, her mother, her eight children, and whatever relatives or friends needed a place to stay.

She exhorted us to get an education, using herself as an example of someone who could have gone much further if she had stayed in school. "I'm not afraid to work," she'd remind us, "but without an education I can only get so far." In New York, she managed to be promoted to supervisor in the factories where she started as a seamstress. Her pride in her progress was tempered by her ambition. "Some day," she'd say, "I'd like to have my own factory."

As a teenager, I didn't appreciate Mami's boldness, tenacity, determination. My adolescence was a frustrating tug-of-war between us, as I tried to both live up to her expectations and shred the ties that bound me to her. I admired her courage but seethed against her demands, her constant reminder that, as the eldest, I was an example for my sisters and brothers. Every move I made was scrutinized, not only by Mami, but also by Tata, by Mami's third husband, Don Carlos, by the eight, then nine, then ten other pairs of eyes looking to me for direction. Or so she said and so I believed. By the time I had ten siblings and was ready to start my own life, my sisters and brothers had made it a point *not* to follow my lead.

When I moved away from our Puerto Rican neighborhoods in search of what I couldn't find there, they stayed. Perhaps they saw how hard it was to integrate the me away from home to the me that plodded up the stairs every day, exhausted and irritable. Maybe they wanted to avoid the struggle to live between two cultures—a struggle that I was afraid to lose and afraid to win. It's possible that they simply did not care to take on Mami's ambitions. Little by little, my five sisters and five brothers left her to form their own families alongside spouses who had to compete with a formidable mother-in-law. That might partly account for the fact that, so far, we eleven siblings have had twenty-four spouses between us.

One day, as we were slumped around the television, Mami stiffened, stared at the screen. "What are they doing?" she said, her voice strained. In grainy black-and-white images, women about my age, dressed very much the way I did, were burning bras over an open fire. "Why are they doing that?" Mami asked, in a panic. It was as I explained the concept behind bra burning to Mami that I came to understand irony. The bra, which women of my generation were burning as a symbol of their liberation, was, for my mother, a livelihood, symbolic of her ability to provide for her eleven children and elderly mother.

Eight years after we arrived in the United States, Mami managed to buy a house in one of the most depressed parts of Brooklyn. It was on the first floor of our house on Fulton Street that Mami set up her very own "*fábrica,*" where she worked alongside her other employees—her mother, her aunt, and a cousin. We were forbidden to enter it. She didn't think we should depend on factories for a living. New York's garment manufacturing industry was moving to other parts of the world; some firms were even settling in Puerto Rico. She took in piecework for the smaller companies that couldn't afford gigantic factories in Singapore or Mexico. Eventually, this kind of work dried up too. She had to give up her factory and sell her house.

The failure of her business drove Mami out of New York. She had separated from Don Carlos, so she returned to Puerto Rico, where she thought she could start over using what she had learned in the United States. She brought Tata with her and nursed her through the withdrawal from the daily beer and wine that had incapacitated her most of her adult life.

By the time my family retreated to the island, I was living in Texas, with a man a year older than Mami. She had stopped talking to me, or perhaps I had stopped talking to her. By running away with him, I managed to exchange her demands for his. By the time I realized my mistake, it was too late. Trapped in an unhappy relationship, I was ashamed to seek what I needed most—my mother's protective bosom.

It would be five years before I saw her again. In that time, Mami married and divorced a man I never met, and then married a widower we'd known years earlier when we first lived in Macún. She had returned to the barrio where she had been miserable, to a cement house not far from where the public fountain had stood. She had learned to drive, had bought a wine-colored Cadillac, which my sisters and brothers christened "*la ballena,*" the whale.

"Why a Cadillac?" I asked.

"I need a big car because I have a big family," she answered. She still had six of her own children at home as well as her husband's five teenagers.

I missed my family during the time I was estranged from them, with only an occasional letter or Christmas card. Years later, as my younger siblings recalled those days, I was filled with nostalgia for the chaotic, crisis-driven existence which I'd tried so desperately to escape. But one phone call from Mami and I was grateful that, painful as it was, I'd managed to flee the day-to-day drama of her life.

She lived in Macún, then in Dorado, then in Bayamón, where she raised the rest of her children and her husband's. Tata developed diabetes and one of her legs had to be amputated. As the younger children graduated from high school, Mami took care of Tata, who was in and out of hospitals with one ailment or another. She attended to her through every illness, until she was as depleted and in need of care as Tata herself. After one frantic phone call, I flew to Puerto Rico to take over the nightly watch Mami thought necessary to keep Tata alive. Thin and in obvious pain, Tata was, nevertheless, alert. With Mami still in the room, she appealed to me.

"Everyone I know is gone, I'm in pain. I have nothing to do." She gazed with sad, exhausted eyes toward her daughter. "The only reason I stick around is because you won't let me die."

"Ay, *Tata, déjate de tonterías,*" Mami said, dismissing Tata's words with a wave of the hand, turning away to wipe her tears. Tata looked at me and grinned.

"She doesn't like it when I tell her the truth," she croaked.

Mami ministered to Tata through her final illness. She died in Mami's arms, in the room filled with the relics of her long life, the photographs of her great-grandchildren, and—even though she was not Catholic and never went to church—a small altar to the Virgin, decorated with rosaries and plastic carnations. She wore her one good dress to the grave.

A few months after Tata died, Mami learned that her husband was having an affair with a younger woman. Their divorce was nasty and, coming on the heels of her mother's death, it completely unhinged Mami, so that we worried about her mental health. She alternated fits of crying with crazy-eyed rants about how much she'd suffered in her life and how, no matter how hard she worked, things always blew up in her face. Her children had left home, her mother was dead, her ex-husband paraded his big-buttocked *chilla* around the old neighborhood so as to humiliate her. It was too much for Mami, who, for the first time in her life, was living alone and had no one to care for but herself.

My sisters and brothers and I made and received long, sob-filled phone calls in which we tried our best to show Mami the brighter side of life. We pointed to her now grown and independent children, to her seventeen grandchildren, to the upcoming birthdays, weddings, Christmas holidays. Norma, who lived in the same neighborhood, came by frequently to sit with her. Papi also came by, and was a better friend than he had been a husband. He and Norma made more than one emergency visit to Mami after neighbors called to say they'd heard her sobbing loudly in the rooms devoid of people.

We took turns visiting her, or had her stay with us for weeks at a time. When she came to visit me, she spent her entire stay cleaning and cooking, happy to have someone to look after. By then, I was married and, unable to ignore the longing that increased with every birthday, I had given birth to two children, whom Mami spoiled as only a grandmother can. More than once she told me I'd gotten off easy, that my two well-behaved children together didn't give me as much trouble as I had given her. By then we could laugh about it, although a twinge of guilt still pricked the edges of my conscience.

It took her a couple of years to get over the ill-timed betrayal by her ex-husband. But she persevered and, finding whatever reserves of resilience and optimism were still left, she smiled again and began making plans. But she swore never again to have anything to do with men. After five husbands, she says she has given relationships as good a chance as anyone can, only to be disappointed. That hasn't stopped men from trying. Last year a suitor courted her for a few months before she put an end to it. "What do I want with some *viejo* whose underwear I have to scrub?" she asked rhetorically. "I'm fine the way things are."

Eventually, all but one of my sisters and brothers moved to the United States with their families. For a few months, Mami bounced back and forth between New York and Puerto Rico, spending time with one or another of us. One day, her friend Ursula invited Mami to accompany her on vacation to Florida, where Ursula had a mobile home. She took Mami to Disney World and SeaWorld, to gleaming shopping malls, to cheerful Sunday-afternoon pig roasts organized by Puerto Ricans newly arrived in Central Florida. They went on a cruise to nowhere, and, when they returned, Mami called to tell me that she was buying Ursula's mobile home with the money from her divorce settlement.

She called to inform, not to ask an opinion. Still, I tried to dissuade her. A trailer in Florida was the last place I imagined Mami could find happiness. It didn't occur to me that happiness was not what she hoped for when she moved to a city in a state where she didn't know anyone. "*Lo que yo necesito es tranquilidad*," she said, which is what I had sought as an adolescent.

Mami wants to remove herself from the daily crises of her extended family. "I'm an old woman," she insists. "I raised you. Now it's time for you to take care of yourselves and leave me be."

But we don't believe that she really wants us to leave her alone. When we're sick, we call to sniff and cough into her ear until she promises to come take care of us. If a relationship fails, we camp out in the tiny room at one end of her trailer and crawl out when the kitchen smells of oregano and garlic. If school is out and the kids have nothing to do, Mami is enlisted to traipse with them through Disney World.

We circle her like bees around a flower, unable to let her go in much the same way she couldn't let go of Tata. We constantly complain to one another about her eccentricities and startling prejudices, just as we take for granted her generosity, capacity for love, and ability to overlook her children's shortcomings while she criticizes the same behavior in others.

Her adventurous spirit has not diminished as she enters her seventieth year. Last week Mami called because a woman she just met wants to sell her a condo in a town none of us have ever heard of in Southeast Florida. The big attraction, besides the asking price, seems to be that the condo is in an area not often hit by tornadoes. If she can sell her trailer, and if, between all eleven children we can contribute to the mortgage, she can buy it.

"But Mami," I protest. "The condo is in a town you've never even visited."

"So what? It's not like I haven't done that before," she reminds me.

"But there are hurricanes in South Florida."

"And haven't I been through dozens of them in Puerto Rico?"

Sometimes when she calls, I'm afraid to come to the phone, wondering what fabulous opportunity or new crisis will be at the other end, breathless. She speaks softly at first, but then her voice rises, and I can almost see the flushed cheeks and bright eyes, the hands gesticulating as she tries to describe her latest obsession.

It's exhausting to be her child. But it was such passion and boldness that led her, on a stormy August day, to give herself to Papi. I imagine her then as I see her now, brimming with excitement at the sheer possibility of life, eager to turn toward where the next moment will take her. She could not have known how hard it would be to raise eleven children under unimaginable conditions. Even though I was there, I'm still amazed we all survived and have managed to form families of our own. Through the years, her life has served as both an example of what we should avoid and what we should aspire to. It is her generous spirit, courage, creativity, and dignity that I, her firstborn, try to emulate, her lessons written on every page of my life.

María Amparo Palomino in her early thirties

The photograph was published in several magazines and newspapers sometime in the late sixties, when this mami was chosen one of the most beautiful women in Mexico. The author, María Amparo Escandón, is the eighth in a long line of María Amparos.

꙰ ꙰ ꙰ ꙰ MARÍA AMPARO ESCANDÓN

María Amparo Escandón was born in Mexico City. She is the author of a novel, Esperanza's Box of Saints *(Scribners), and the screenplay for the film* Santitos, *both based on a short story originally published in* Prairie Schooner. *She lives in Los Angeles where she teaches at the UCLA Extension Writer's Program.*

My Mother in the Nude

My mother doesn't cook. She never has. Not once. Forget ironing, vacuuming, making the bed. Those chores are simply not part of her life. She won't do them. Not even to impress my father. She can barely recall the color of her kitchen. "Is it off-white? Or was that the kitchen in the house on Sierra Candela? Why are you asking me this? Don't tell me you're going to write about me, you little tattletale."

I used to have to wake her up when I came home from school. She wasn't lazy. She just lived on European time. Starting the day at two in the afternoon with breakfast in bed seemed reasonable after having stayed up reading until five in the morning the night before. She read everything, from Kant's philosophical doctrine to *Reader's Digest's* moralistic anecdotes. While my father snored by her side, mumbling every so often and pleading with her to turn out the lights, she'd study whatever she could in lieu of the college education she hadn't gotten. She didn't need one. Or at least that had been her family's belief when she married at age nineteen: girls didn't need a degree to be house-wives.

But my mother was no ordinary girl. Still, for a number of years she tried to behave like one, which was the same as trying to fit a size-ten foot into size-seven shoes. She had friends. They got together for coffee and pastries in the afternoons and talked about diapers and nannies. They played cards. They did each other's makeup. They went shopping. They went to the movies. They organized parties every weekend, always leaving the mess for the maid to clean up the next morning. In the sixties, young mothers in Mexican society were expected to do just that. My mother did the expected and did it well, especially looking beautiful and going shopping. But she refused to waste her money on dinnerware, appliances, sheets, or pots and pans. "Why get a new toaster for the cook to enjoy?" She always looked as if she came out of a Saks Fifth Avenue window, but her household items looked as if they came from a thrift shop.

When my brothers and I were children, my mother liked to dress us as if we were triplets. Identical outfits for the three of us. If my brothers' pants were gray, so was my skirt. Same shirts, too. The problem was that Javier couldn't stay clean for more than one hour, so every time my mother would notice that he was dirty, she'd change us all into clean clothes. Because Julio and I were quite neat, we hated that. But our opinion was not something that interested her.

Department-store clothes have never been good enough for my mother. She can't get a suit off the rack without changing the buttons, adding shoulder pads or doing some other sort of alteration. In her early twenties, she signed up for a class in haute couture and learned to dress herself like a Dior model. She also made most of my clothes. Even in my dreams, I'd hear the hum of the sewing machine in the next room. Sometimes, she'd wake me up in the middle of the night to try on a dress. Half asleep, I'd make every effort to keep my balance, oftentimes poking myself with a pin. "A pinprick is good luck," she'd say. "Just don't get any blood on the fabric." When I made my First Holy Communion, she sewed all night and finished my gown one hour before the ceremony, just in time for the maid to iron it and for me to put it on and run to church. Everyone thought it was beautiful.

Making her own clothes didn't diminish my mother's obsession for shopping. Twice a year the entire family drove from Mexico City to Brownsville, Texas, returning with four suitcases full of new clothes. American clothes. Mexican clothes were worthless. "They come apart at the hands of the laundry woman. They fade. They're ugly. There's no style to them." We'd set off north in a caravan, my family and perhaps a couple of my aunts and uncles with their children, to conquer the stores of the closest border town. Once on the way back, the luggage fell off our station wagon's roof rack somewhere near Ciudad Victoria. My brother Julio was the first to notice the loose cords whipping around in the wind and hitting the back window. My mother almost strangled my uncle Álvaro right there, in the middle of the road. "He's no good. Why did I let him tie down the suitcases?" We went back and spent the entire day looking for scattered clothes along the road, but we didn't find even the tiniest sock.

Sometimes we'd go all the way to Houston to shop. Now *that* was fun. While my mother spent the day at the Galleria trying on clothes for the next season, my dad would take us to the Six

Flags amusement park or, better yet, to the Astrodome. In Brownsville, where there wasn't much to do, we had to follow my mother around, squeeze ourselves into little fitting rooms and watch her try on eight skirts and twelve blouses. All we could do at the stores was get in trouble. One day my brother Julio and my cousin Pepe accidentally knocked over a huge stack of shoeboxes, burying themselves under the pile. My mother pretended not to know them, grabbed me by the arm and walked out of the store, leaving the six-year-old children behind to deal with the situation.

M oney was never any object for my mother. "Coins are round to roll away and bills are made out of paper to be swept away by the wind," she'd say. She would stay in a mall spending every cent she had until closing time or, as once happened in Miami, after closing time. The department store closed for the day while she was busy in a fitting room. When she came out at 11:00 p.m. with at least seven outfits in hand, the lights had been dimmed, the salespeople were nowhere to be found, and the doors' iron curtains had been rolled down. But she has always been resourceful, so she looked for a pay phone and called 911 so the police would come and let her out. While she waited for them to get there and locate the store's security guard, she hung the clothes she had chosen on a rack behind the cash register and attached a Terminator-like notice written on a shopping bag: "Do not re-stock. I'll be back." My father, who had been desperately looking for her for hours, had to take her back to the store as soon as it opened in the morning. She paid for the garments she'd selected the night before and continued shopping where she had left off.

The Galleria in Houston was her favorite mall. My brothers

and I loved it, too, because it had a spectacular ice-skating rink on the lower level, so we didn't have to worry about when my mother would pick us up. We'd just go round and round the rink until she appeared, laden with shopping bags. We stayed at the hotel next door so as not to waste valuable time commuting to the mall.

One day, when my mother was all done at the Galleria, she decided she'd hit another mall across town. After the hotel's valet brought the rental car, she sped off with my aunt Tinina in the passenger seat. A few minutes later, while looking for a map, they found an umbrella that neither of them recognized. They had taken the wrong car. But my mother wasn't about to turn back, no matter how much my aunt begged, pleaded, even threatened her. It was no use. "So what if this is the States? What can they do? Sue us? It's the hotel's fault," my mother said. She could not possibly afford to turn around and waste time. It was the last day before we had to go back to Mexico and she still had plenty of shopping to do. So she continued on her quest, now in a stolen vehicle and with a kidnapped aunt. When they arrived at the other mall, she called the hotel and suggested they lend her rental car to the lady whose car she had taken, since she wouldn't be back until that evening. The hotel had to scramble and rent yet another car for the other woman. Life at the mall can be exciting with my mother.

She no longer goes to Houston. She shops in Los Angeles, where I live. Fortunately for her, there are two major shopping centers within walking distance of my house. Unfortunately for the rest of the family, we don't get to see her unless we follow her around. Every time she comes to visit, she asks me to take her to a museum, but on the way we make a quick stop at the mall and, of course, stay there the rest of the day, leaving the Van Goghs for another occasion.

Over the years I've learned to understand her obsession with appearance, particularly when it comes to the clothes she wears. She has confessed to not having had enough as a girl. "Your grandma was very austere. She only bought me a couple of dresses for each season." So, in her adult life, she has over-compensated. Before I lost track, I once counted one hundred and thirty-four sweaters in her closet. Forty-six pairs of shoes. Sixty-eight skirts. Seventy-nine dresses. Fifty-seven business suits. Thirty-three purses. Twenty-six pairs of sunglasses. Twelve coats. Sixty-one pairs of pants. Nine wigs. Seventeen jackets. Twenty-one evening gowns. Thirteen swimsuits. Three drawers full of makeup. Forty-two bras. One pair of designer jeans. When her clothes go out of style, she gives them to her maid or to some charity, then goes shopping to replenish her wardrobe for the next season.

My mother also buys clothes for me, for my children, and for my husband. When I was about to get married, she insisted that I come to my new relationship with a brand-new wardrobe. "You definitely need a trousseau. Who wants a newlywed in old rags?" We flew to Houston where she bought three possible evening gowns to wear at my wedding. She'd make her final choice depending on the weather the day of the ceremony. Because she was so focused on picking her own clothes, it was easy to convince her to give me the money she had allocated for me. I'd shop on my own and we'd meet at the end of the day. When I came back to the hotel room that night, carrying only one little bag containing a fabulous Leica 35 mm camera with all sorts of lenses and cases, she stopped talking to me until two days after we'd returned from Houston. But it was worth it. The camera was the best thing I could have taken on my honeymoon.

Because she is the expert, my mother feels she is in charge of making everyone else's clothing decisions. "Your brother Javier can't coordinate a shirt with a pair of pants. I have to shop for him," she tells me. Never mind the fact that my brother Javier is a forty-year-old orthopedic surgeon who is, I'm sure, capable of dressing himself. "He can't even pick the right color for a surgery gown." Still, he plays along and lets my mother decide.

As a little girl, I had no choice. My mother determined what I wore every day. She picked the clothes the night before and laid them on my bed. I endured the cute knit socks, the ample slips stiff with starch, the pretty dresses, and the bows. When I became a teenager, the logical step was to rebel against her where it hurt the most, so I tried dressing like the rest of my peers, starting a mother-daughter battle that lasted for many years. But since she was still buying all of my clothes, the battle was quite futile. I was able to save enough money to buy myself a couple of things that I deeply cherished, like a pair of jeans (my only pair), the ones with peace signs embroidered on the bell bottoms and a Rolling Stones tongue on the back pocket. One day my mother burned them in the middle of the back yard as a symbol of her victory. From then on I was allowed to wear only tailor-made jeans, if any at all. And forget the Levi's overalls. "Those god-awful potato sacks make you look like Diego Rivera."

In my mother's life, appearance is not just about clothes. "To be beautiful, you must suffer," she's told me countless times. In her relentless pursuit of physical perfection, she has spent thousands of hours in front of a mirror analyzing her naked self, painstakingly fixing her hair and applying makeup with the precision of an aerospace engineer. "There are no natural beauties. You must work hard to look good." As a child I understood this as a curse cast upon women by some creature who didn't like us. Why didn't my dad have to suffer? All he did was shave his face in two minutes. That's how long it took my mother to apply one false eyelash. I promised myself that I would never wear makeup, but as I reached my teenage years, not only did I fail to keep my promise, but my mother's emphasis on beauty and its importance was confirmed every month when I leafed through the pages of *Seventeen* magazine. I realized then that the skinny American girls in the ads—all blond, all with perfect smiles and no pimples—owned the world. So I suffered. Without asking my opinion, my mother put me on a diet, took me to the orthodontist, subjected me to painful facials, straightened my naturally curly hair, and did anything else she could do to correct my shortcomings.

At first I tried to meet her expectations, but I knew I didn't have the natural resources. Otherwise, why would she be so persistent in improving my looks? As a girl, I was too skinny. As a teenager, I was too fat. "You're just at an ungraceful age," she'd say to me, no matter how old I was.

Then, when I started college—finally, my own life—she decided to enroll, as well. She was the most beautiful and well-dressed thirty-eight-year-old student on my college campus. I still remember all those seniors, crazy over her, who would sit close to her in the cafeteria. She'd wear the tightest size-six pants and a hairdo Farrah Fawcett would've killed for. When I had to turn in a group project, all my guy friends wanted to be on my team so that they could come to my house and get a close look at my mother. In contrast, I took the post-hippie route. I wore those Mexican leather sandals that have soles made out of old car tires, long wrinkled cotton skirts, and colorful Oaxacan *huipiles*. I let my naturally curly hair go. No longer able to force me to wear what she wanted, my mother spent quite a lot of time talking to me about how people must dress well to succeed in life. We graduated together. She was class valedictorian.

My mother went on to get a second degree and, unlike her friends, a job. She was the most aggressive, most beautiful and best-dressed professional training executive in the Mexican Chamber of the Construction Industry (where I also worked as their magazine's editor). I was already married by then, but sometimes my mother and I would ride together to the office. On the way, we'd talk about our work and, needless to say, about how to dress for success. And she should know. In the years that followed, due to her intelligence—and, according to her, aided by her wardrobe—she became the Mexican government's ultimate authority in the professional training and productivity fields, introducing disciplines such as "zero defects" into the national corporate culture.

There is not one day when my mother doesn't look dazzling in a perfect outfit, impeccable makeup and hairdo, no wrinkles (on clothes or face), and an ever-fresh manicure. Yet her drawers are a mess. Her finances are chaos. And she is always late, shamefully late. But no one seems to care. She is too charming for these things to matter. People just want to be around her. I wonder what she learned from a mother who (according to her) was far more beautiful than she. I also wonder what I've learned from having had a mother who values physical beauty as much as she does. What legacy I will pass along to my own daughter that women's magazines and Calvin Klein ads don't pass along already? How many of us are coming to terms with this issue in our therapists' offices? I wonder.

I have slowly taken charge of the way I look and how I feel about my personal appearance, years after I put one thousand five hundred and seventy-two miles between my mother and me. Cutting the umbilical cord was easier than I thought. I have a couple of pairs of jeans in my closet. I let my daughter wear whatever she wants and give my opinion only when she asks me. I very seldom visit a shopping center. And to keep things simple, I wear mostly black.

Mandalit with her mother,
Dolores del Barco Villarreal,
Lima, Peru, 1963

*"And you'll join in the long line of family women
who have had the strength to overcome adversity,
explore new lands, and make a home for themselves
in hostile environments."*

Mandalit del Barco is a reporter for National Public Radio and a frequent contributor to NPR's Latino USA and Latina magazine. Born in Lima, Peru, she grew up in Kansas and California. She has reported for the Miami Herald and The Village Voice, WNYC-FM, and WBAI-FM. This essay was written as the author prepared for a Fulbright grant in Peru, following in her mother's footsteps.

"Hello, Dollinks"
Letters from Mom

"And in the morning, we found the custodian lashed to the Xerox machine, slowly going back and forth, back and forth . . ."

The idea was for Mom to think up a satirical mystery set in an inner-city public school, starring her as the teacher/detective who solves crimes. This is the first line she came up with.

"Sort of like a copycat murder, huh, Mom?"

"Yes, the *Duplicating Room Mystery*. The traditional venue for knockdown, dragout fights in any school. You know how it is. Everyone must have use of the copy machine immediately if not sooner. Well, I've noticed that duplicating-fluid cans have the warning label 'Cannot Be Made Non-Poisonous.' Once I saw, in a faculty room, a can of the fluid temptingly located on a shelf near the coffeepot. I thought, 'Aw, gee, that's terrible.' I had to move it away, but I always thought that would make a good element for a mystery story."

"What else?"

"Well, there are so many potential victims. How to choose? There's the overbearing teacher, the whiny teacher, the entire P.E. department . . ."

See, my mom is an avid reader of mystery novels and science fiction tales. Our entire TV room (in which she and Dad watch her favorite British mystery on public television, *Rumpole of the Bailey*) is covered wall-to-wall with bookshelves, crammed three-deep with paperbacks, each of which she's read and re-read at least four times. There simply are not enough mystery and sci-fi stories written to satisfy her literary hunger. Falling asleep with a paperback in her hands, then waking in the middle of the night to devour another, she's like a very well-read *Chupalibros*.

Since before my brother and I were born, she's also been a teacher. A very good teacher. A very good and gentle and witty teacher, who is often amused by the comical situations in which she finds herself. After having taught kindergartners in Peru and college students in Kansas, she began a three-decade-long (so far) career in urban public schools. Over the years as a bilingual education teacher and specialist, as an assistant high-school principal, a middle-school principal, and an administrator now in charge of the district's International Baccalaureate Program, she's had lots of fun collecting stories of her own, both real and imagined.

For starters, there were the students' names. Female (pronounced fe-MALL-ee). Tortillas (ta-TEE-yuz). Her mother, my grandmother—had been one of the first English as a Second Language teachers in California, starting at a public elementary school in the late 1960s—she also taught some doozies, such as the twins Latanya and Lasagna.

Then there's the fact that schools—particularly middle- and senior-high schools—are such fertile settings for high drama and situation comedy. Mom has cheered at more basketball and football games, chaperoned more junior and senior proms, attended more board meetings and student funerals, than anyone I've met. She's survived budget cuts, battles over methodology, and teachers "with the critical judgment of a gerbil." In the ever-changing political environment in California, she heroically championed bilingual education. (She even wrote her Ph.D. dissertation on the subject while she was teaching full-time!) Through it all, she's kept her sense of humor.

"Of all the lousy gin joints in all the lousy towns, why did he have to pick our high school?" began one short story she wrote for our family's amusement. "We should have known. It *was* a dark and stormy day when he first showed up for the interview. But then, how could we know? It's always dark in that building. However, at the time, all we were aware of was that a tall, blond, extremely handsome and personable man was interested in teaching at our school.

" 'Languages,' he said. 'I'm from Yugoslavia.' We could have, perhaps, picked up a clue from his perfect smile (which tended to sag at the corners because of the slightly elongated upper canines). But we didn't, and he was hired. He was charming!

"It really wasn't until October (after the first statistical report and consolidations were complete) that we began to wonder a bit. Here was a teacher who volunteered to supervise games at night; who took pleasure in working until dark (outside—who could tell from inside?); who liked to hang around the school till all hours; whose students were indeed soon speaking a foreign language: agglutinogen, hemoglobin, sanguine.

"The fact that he seemed to prefer black for his wardrobe we attributed to mourning for his homeland under Communist rule. (He had left in the early 1940s, when he was two.) Wrapping himself in a cape we put down to eccentricity. The increasing pallor of the students in his classes went almost undetected amid the tension before SAT tests and college application deadlines.

"As time went on, however, we did begin to notice that, in conversation, he was only capable of biting remarks or incisive comments. But we didn't probe too deeply into his gushing assertions . . .

"It was really a moment of insight on our part that occurred during the annual basketball tournament. (Funny what several successive nights of interminable basketball games, doughnuts, and strong coffee can inspire.) We finally realized that what he had really said during his interview was, 'Languishing. I mine jugulars.' "

Mom's letters to me and my brother Andy were not always about vampires, but they did usually begin, "Hello, dollinks!" Sometimes, they're addressed, "*Wawachaykuna*" (that means "my beloved babies" in Quechua, the Andean language Dad grew up speaking and taught to Peace Corps volunteers). And over the years, her dispatches have chronicled the random goings-on at school, the false fire alarms, flooded hallways, cheap cafeteria food, fifth-period hall walkers, and club fundraisers: "M&M sales are up (both plain and peanut)."

Sometimes, her letters would detail the maddening bureaucracy typical of any institution. (Her observations remind me at times of scenes from the film *Brazil*.) For example:

". . . About 10:00, the electricians finally came to see about the computer hook-up that we requested in August 1997. They met up with the two painters who showed up to follow a work order from 1994. To round out the trades, we also had the plumbers who came to 'see' about the flood, and the ceiling tilers who were there to fix the tiles that are either missing or have fallen on the students in various classrooms over the years. The usual procedure is for a work order to be sent in. Then, several months later, two persons from the appropriate union show up to see what needs to be done. A few months after this, two others show up to 'measure' what needs to be done. They then go off with the figures and are never seen again. Sometimes—although this is not too likely, even within the same year—someone else comes out and actually fixes things."

Other letters included incidents that set her and her best friend, a colleague and high-school principal, off into fits of girlish giggles:

"Yesterday was fun," one letter begins, "Calvin, the resident rabbit who inhabits the sixth-grade wing, and is usually to be found in Mr. Z's room, had a visitor. Armando brought his rabbit to visit. Calvin was instantly smitten, and proceeded to romance and swiftly to 'carnal lust' right in the room with all the sixth graders. Of course, instruction in ancient cultures wasn't as interesting, so an impromptu biology lesson took place. Unfortunately, Calvin has been raised by himself and has never really met other rabbits, so it is unlikely that he would know that he was really romancing a male. (Mr. Shirley, perhaps? The hare stylist?) Mr. Z didn't have the heart to tell the kids, because the girls are already planning a baby shower for Armando's rabbit."

Languages and wordplay have always fascinated Mom, who delights in Bugs Bunny cartoons and *Monty Python's Flying Cir-*

cus. She's also always appreciated the cultural mix of students and teachers and parents with whom she works. In the international city where she lives, students in the schools have emigrated from across the globe. Mom has noted that any time there's a war or other calamity in the world (in Central America, Vietnam, Africa) children from that region will show up in the city's public schools two years later. At the high school where Mom taught and worked as an administrator, students spoke twenty-seven different languages.

She likes to tell the story of the time when students at the high school where she was vice principal were playing touch football on the field at lunchtime. "And this one Cambodian kid ran into this American kid who was huge. He was on the football team. Real nice kid, but big. And this Cambodian kid was carrying the football and he ran into the bigger kid and knocked himself out. The big kid hadn't laid a glove on him. He was just standing there and—WHACK!—the other kid ran into him.

"So we got the nurse out there to check on the kid (at that time there was still such a thing as a school nurse). And because he'd been knocked out, she had to ask the traditional questions:

" 'Where are you?'

" 'Uh, on the ground.'

"WRONG! He had failed to name which city he was in.

" 'Second question: Who's the president?'

"Well, the kid didn't know, having just arrived in this country!

"So the nurse called the ambulance for him. She figured he had a concussion."

⨏ ⨏ ⨏

S he prefaces another of her favorite stories with the cau-
tion to remember that none of the kids spoke English.
None of them!

"Charming little vignette at school the other day," she
wrote. "Seems that Nguyen, from Vietnam, was making eyes at,
and gave what he later insisted was a 'compliment' to the beautiful Filipino girl in his English as a Second Language class.

"To wit: 'Hey, baby, nice chest.'

"She was insulted, and complained to Manuel, from Mexico,
and Chantha, from Cambodia, also in the class. They then felt
they had to defend the lady's honor, like knights-errant, whatever the century, and got into a fight with Nguyen, in the hall, of
course, which is where things got a bit complicated. Because
then Farah, from Somalia, felt he had to help defend the kid in
his math class (Nguyen) and who knows what language all of
this took place in, because none of the above even have a rudimentary knowledge of English in common." Later, as we tried to
sort the whole thing out in the office, we sent for the girl whose
beautiful figure had caused all the excitement. After a while, the
security guard came back and said, "I don't know what you people mean by 'really built,' but this is the girl." And behind him
was a girl whose figure, as my friend the principal kindly
described it, was "an ironing board."

There are other incidents, even more scandalous, that I've
sworn not to tell in print. What makes them hilarious—beyond
the stories themselves—is that Mom relates them with such rel-
ish. She giggles. Her face turns beet red. She is, in fact, a very
mild-mannered woman, a former Girl Scout camp leader who
embarrasses easily. ("You gotta remember I grew up in the last
century," she jokes, meaning the nineteenth century, meaning

she was raised in the Midwest with old-fashioned values.) She wears eyeglasses and calf-length skirts and sensible flat shoes. In visiting students at their homes or on her way to school events, she has walked through gangland turf, unscathed. The tough guys defer to her. She's often mistaken for a nun (a thought that makes her and my Dad snicker). She and her similarly attired best friend, the school principal, used to use the joke names Nun Such and Nun of the Above.

She's no nun, although I do sometimes think of her as a saint, sacrificing so much of her time and energy and money for her family; staying up nights to help Dad or to help me and Andy with our term papers; scraping together money to pay the bills and send us to expensive universities; as well as caring deeply for her students. While she may delight in some of the silly scenarios she's witnessed, that's not what she finds most important in her work. She has a great deal of affection for her students and her colleagues, and she rejoices when she sees someone teaching well, thinking how lucky those students are (and remembering fondly the teachers who made a difference in her life, too).

Just as she beams when she's asked about her family, she's also proud of the National Merit Scholars her inner-city schools have produced, the kids with the perfect 1600 scores on their SATs, the students from all over the world who arrived speaking no English and went on to become valedictorians before attending Ivy League universities with full scholarships. Some of her students are now doctors, lawyers, engineers, firefighters, police officers, teachers.

Mom hadn't really set out to be a teacher (though nearly everyone else in the family has become a teacher as well); she wanted to be an anthropologist. A folklorist, to be specific. Teaching was a fascinating way for her to make a living, and she found she was good at it. When Andy and I were young, she somehow found time to research and trace for us the family trees of her Mexican-American family in the United States and Dad's family in Peru. She hung up old family photos in our dining room. I still remember accompanying her as she visited all the older relatives. Using an old reel-to-reel tape recorder, she recorded their memories.

I guess it's in the genes; I find myself now as a radio journalist, recording stories of people's lives (albeit these days with a mini disc recorder). And I'm following Mom's footsteps in Peru, also on a Fulbright grant. When she was there in the early 1960s, she chronicled the folktales of the Andean region around Ayacucho. Besides her own close encounters, she documented Quechua stories about wandering ghosts / condemned spirits, like the Manchachiku ("the one who frightens") and about animal transformations, such as Xarxacha (the people who become llamas at night), or the Ukuku (the bear / person).

As I prepared to leave for Peru, inspired by Mom, and with the hope of following up on her research more than thirty-five years later, I received from her a gift: a beautifully handwritten letter that touched my soul and made me weep. In it, she tells me how proud she and my father are. And she offers this:

"So now you'll go off on a great adventure, and you'll join in the long line of family women who have had the strength to overcome adversity, explore new lands, and make a home for themselves in hostile environments. The women in our family have always been strong (as exemplified by your great-great-great-great-great-grandmother in the late 1700s, who loaded up her babies into carrying baskets and rode through the nights to escape the Apaches, while going to settle in Chihuahua. Or your great-great-aunt Preciliana Palacios who took over the care of her younger brothers and sister and set out from Chihuahua to the U.S. in 1898, to make a better life for them away from a dictatorship, or your great-great-great-grandmother Petronilia Saez del Barco, who faced down the Chilean soldiers in the War of the Pacific in the 1880s in Ayacucho, on behalf of the towns-people . . ."

The letter goes on. I will treasure it forever. My mom—who still plays piano duets with me (we both laugh with astonishment if we manage to finish on the right note and at the same time); who took Andy and me with her to antiwar rallies and women's-lib meetings and political campaigns when we were small; who made us believe we could do and be anything we wanted; who encouraged me to go to the university and graduate school to be a journalist and work for NPR and later to apply for the Fulbright; who never criticized and is always supportive—has been the greatest teacher of all to her own children. She's passed on to us the love she and my father share, our family folklore, and her own tales about the worlds she's known. She has taught us how to be storytellers, puns and all.

The Sea of Puerto Rico

Isabel Oliveras Quijano,
mother of Alba Ambert

"I am sitting in the ocean of her lap . . . I revel in her aroma
of sand and palm fronds and milk."

༄ ༄ ༄ ༄ ༄ ༄ ༄ ༄ ༄ ༄ ALBA AMBERT

Alba Ambert was born in San Juan, Puerto Rico, and brought up in the South Bronx. Her novel A Perfect Silence *(Arte Público Press) won the Carey McWilliams Award, and her novel* Porque hay silencio *(Arte Público Press) won the Literature Award of the Instituto de Literatura Puertorriqueña for best novel. Other works include* The Eighth Continent and Other Stories *(Arte Público Press), four poetry collections, several books for children, and the oral history* Every Greek Has a Story *(Athens College Press). She is a frequent contributor to literary reviews and anthologies. She is the recipient of the 1997 President's Award of the Massachusetts Association for Bilingual Education. A Writer-in-Residence at Richmond, The American International University in London, she has recently completed her third novel and is at work on her next book. She divides her time between London and San Juan.*

Persephone's Quest at Waterloo: A Daughter's Tale

At Waterloo Station, the train rumbles to a stop and a loud-speaker voice garbles, "Mind the gap!" I step forward and face the black span between the train and the edge of the platform. My head spins. My shoes are packed with lead. Commuters swarm in and out of the car. Still, I can't move. "Mind the gap!" the disembodied voice warns again. The darkness in that forbidding gap looms wide as a boundless ocean. I am utterly helpless. A loud clank fills the air and the doors shut in my face. I am stranded at the empty platform, like a castaway on a deserted island. I look out at the litter-strewn rail pit and back up slowly.

In the end, I manage to board a train home. The engine gathers speed, but at the other side of the platform the Eurostar hurtles past us to more romantic destinations. The wisp of Brussels and Lille and Paris dissipates in my mind and I am left with a view of the gray Thames and the smoke from industrial chimneys that curls into the leaden sky. In a tiny backyard, a blue dress floats on a clothesline and it is this dress, the way the patch of sea blue cuts against the grayness of the day, the folds unfurling gently like petals in the wind, that engulfs me with a familiar wave of nostalgia. I recall Ionesco, that chronicler of human isolation and chaos, and his woeful summation of his work. "I write out of anguish," he said, "out of nostalgia . . . a nostalgia which no longer knows its object." Looking at the sky-blue dress, I recognize the transcendent feeling that haunts without discernible reason, the symptoms there, the causes well disguised. A nostalgia for something lost so far in the past it's like the faint aroma left in a room after a woman walks out. This is the feeling that so often overwhelms me when I least expect it; the indefinable yearning that has no name. It could be brought on by the scent of jasmine, the sweet-sharp taste of passion fruit, turning a hand over to examine the lifelines. Or it could be summoned by the melody of a bolero or the way a leaf darkens and dies. Greeks have a word for this feeling, untranslatable into English: *kaimos*. "I have *kaimos*," they say with a sigh when a feeling of loss overpowers them, when they are swept by a nostalgia for someone or something lost but not forgotten. *Kaimos* is a pain that is pleasurable because it reminds one of a person or a state of happiness that is no longer there. *Kaimos* is the painful presence of an absence.

I lived in Greece for almost eight years, a stone-etched land steeped in myth and metaphor, where women with names like Aphrodite, Daphne, Phaedra, and Athena abound. Invariably, these women narrated the myths that gave origin to their names. The myths, replete with battles, passions, and jealousies, were captivating. But there was one myth that gripped me as no other—the quintessential mother-daughter myth that, though meant to explain the changes of season, had a more intimate meaning for me. Demeter, the goddess of all that sprouts from the earth, lived with her daughter Persephone. Hades, god of the underworld, fell in love with Persephone. Knowing that her mother would never approve of their marriage, he drove up in a four-horse carriage while Persephone was gathering narcissi and spirited her away to the sunless depths of the earth where he reigned. Not knowing what had happened, a distraught Demeter wandered through the confines of the earth searching for her daughter. In her grief, Demeter neglected the crops and brought famine to the earth. Fearing the end of humanity, Zeus intervened and a bargain was struck. Persephone returned to Demeter, whose happiness at their reunion caused crops to flourish and flowers to bloom once more. But Persephone was forced to return to the underworld for several months each year, bringing periodic grief and desolation to her mother and infertility to the earth.

I have experienced a life of constant change and disruption, my memories are often blurred and indistinct. So I have learned to forge fictions to ford the lacunae of my personal history. Often

I've constructed my own versions of folklore and mythology. The anguish of mother-daughter separation is not unfamiliar to me, and in my rendering of the mother-daughter myth it is Demeter who is snatched to the underworld by Hades and the grief-stricken Persephone who sets out through the vast reaches of the earth in a vigorous quest for her mother. Persephone searches in the eyes of strangers, turns over rocks and boulders, and scrutinizes the flattened moss for signs of her. She stares at the gaps that, like oceans, yawn across every dimension of the earth. She pokes her finger into the cracks in loaves of bread, the tiny pleats in the skin of spoiled grapes. She probes the mold that collects in caves. She calls her mother's name and listens to its resonance on her tongue, hoping for a clue that will explain her disappearance. Every space is prodded and explored. She might be here, she might be there, Persephone murmurs to the wind and moves on, torch in hand, from mountain to seaside, in her indefatigable quest. In my version of the myth, Persephone searches for her mother all her life but never finds her. Though Demeter's loss is devastating, no catastrophes plague the earth. There are no hurricanes, no earthquakes, not a tremor is felt. In the end, nothing happens and Persephone shakes her head in wonder, unable to reconcile her pain with the settled oceans and cloud-misted skies.

M y mother died of tuberculosis when I was two and my life has been defined by that loss. When she died, I was wrapped in a black scarf and driven without warning into exile. Cast from the Garden of Eden, bereft of Lilith and the female oneness I shared with her, I was at an age when the language to express that devastating loss was not available to me. My emotional scaffolding collapsed; for decades afterwards I was unable to attach words to the pain of her absence. Try as I might, I couldn't find the precise expression that would describe the hole that gaped in front of every step I took. For so long I lived without words. Many times I longed to press my finger against her name and feel it harden against my flesh. I was reminded of the author of *Frankenstein*, Mary Wollstonecraft Shelley, whose mother died when she was ten days old. As a small child she would go for walks with her father to the St. Pancras churchyard where her mother, Mary Wollstonecraft, was buried. Her father taught the child to read and spell her name by having her trace the inscription on her mother's stone. One can only imagine the little girl's confusion at reading her own name on her mother's tomb, always searching for her mother in the silence of a grave-yard, haunted by an awareness of her own mortality. This is a common fixation among daughters without mothers that often brings us to the brink of self-destruction and sometimes drives us over that unfathomable edge where, perhaps, we may finally find her.

In this world I'm the only one who remembers my mother, yet I can't remember her. That has been the distinguishing para-dox of my life. Those who would remember her have died, so my mother exists in my mind and no one else's. I'm determined to stoke whatever fragments of her remain in me, make them as vibrant and alive as I can. For I am the memory of my mother. My mind is her altar; a shrine of the intangible. I was too young when she died to remember, but she exists in bits of information I've hoarded through the years, my secret treasure replenished with every word or phrase, said in passing, that might have alluded to her, however tangentially. Hiding in the shadows, I listened avidly as the words rose and fell. I grasped allusions, splinters of events, but never heard the full story. Nor did I dare to ask. With these bits of thread and ribbons of cloth, I've stitched a broad sketch of her life, distant and vague, devoid of the details that would make her life sharp and textured. I will always wonder how much of what I have of her is real and how much imaginary.

Vauxhall, Clapham Junction, Wandsworth Town. The stations flit by with disconcerting familiarity and I hope against the meager evidence available, that my mother's life contained a glimmer of joy, that she was able to hold some dreams for the future. I hope that in the shantytown where she lived and gave birth to me, she owned a bright-blue dress that billowed on a clothesline in the wind and that she carefully pressed it, every Saturday perhaps, with the heavy coal iron she filled from a glowing grill. I hope that on Sundays she was prompted to make the long journey out of the shantytown and across the wide Fernández Juncos and Ponce de León Avenues, down the tree-lined streets tapering to El Condado where the wealthy lived in their white Spanish-colonial houses that sparkled in the sun. She may have struggled across the coconut groves that hugged the shore, her sandaled feet sinking in the sand. Once there, she sat on a blanket, or more likely, a piece of cardboard, while she breathed in the salt-laden air and watched the seagulls dip their beaks in the crests of waves. Then, perhaps flushed from the long walk in the sun, her hand skimmed the water and she poured it over her breasts. But that's just my fantasy. Her Sunday walks were probably to the communal faucet with a water jug on her hip. There were no backyards with clotheslines in the shantytown.

Where did she dry her laundered clothes? I wonder. Did she lift the blood she coughed into her handkerchief with salt? Did she bleach the cloth in the sun? Where did she bathe, wash her hair? Was she disgusted by the roaches and spiders and salamanders that crawled around in the wooden latrine? If there was a latrine. What were her beliefs? Her fears? Her tastes? Did she love mango, as I do, above all other fruit? Did her mouth water when she sliced its golden flesh? Maybe the sweet banana, cheap and plentiful, was her favorite treat. There are so many gaps, so few references to her stunted life. Nothing concrete or tangible exists of her. Not even a photograph. She was buried in a potter's field, so the simple consolation of pressing my finger against her name on a tombstone is unattainable. If I had not been born of her and lived to remember, it would be as if she had never existed. When I die, she will cease to be.

My mother's island is the place where all is settled and defined. A state of perfection. Psychologists say that young children look for a mother in the last place she appeared and that this association of place with mother endures into adulthood. This probably explains my constant need to return to Puerto Rico, the place where I last saw her and where, inexplicably, she disappeared. Despite its limitations, Puerto Rico is my paradise, my womb, the only place where I find true comfort. I no longer have my mother, but I can behold the landscape that was hers: the open sky, the long sparkling arm of the shore, the eye of the sun, the ocean's silver sheen. The island is the place of refuge I frequently leave but that, like Odysseus's Ithaca, I always return to. And as my mother was my eyes and ears and skin when I was an infant, Puerto Rico has been my point of discovery, a stepping stone on a voyage that has taken me far from its shores, while invariably bringing me back in an eternal recurrence that follows the ebb and flow of the tide. Although I recognize its difficulties, this imaginary island-Utopia remains deeply impressed in my being in the same way that my perfect mother endures. My mythical island is as faultless as the mother who lives in my mind. I could never imagine a harsh word from my mother's mouth, or an insincere intent. Had she lived, she would have been flawless, impeccable, perpetually kind and understanding. I had no mother to reassure me when I failed, console me when things went wrong, no mother to tell me that no matter what happened or what I did, I would never forfeit her unconditional love. I know without a doubt that, had she lived, my mother would have been my staunchest supporter and her strength and encouragement would have made life easier. She never would have flagged, nor weakened. My mother would have been an island, full and perfect.

I look out at the church steeple, the construction cranes, and the antennas that streak the horizon. At every station, cautions abound: Do Not Alight Here, Uneven Surface, Do Not Touch Live Rail. When my mother died, I was not only bereft of a voice, but I lived in terrible fear of going blind. I am still amazed at the fact that I can speak without her tongue, feel without her skin, and see without her eyes. Unable to hear the melody of her voice, the only comfort left to me is to speak her language. Spanish, my mother tongue, and the two years we had together, are all that is left. Because my mother tongue is the most tangible thing I possess of her, despite my routine incursions into English, I have clung fiercely to the language that nurtured me when I was an infant and at my most vulnerable. Spanish, mother tongue and mother's tongue, is the coffer that holds the treasure of my mother's voice, her intonation, the gentle cadence of her words. My mother tongue endures in that first precious word she said to me, in the first concept she helped me transform into a word, thus capturing the nature of meaning. It was my mother tongue that allowed me, as an infant, to grasp the meaning of the world that surrounded me. A world that must have seemed so enormous, uncontainable, and hostile, but because of my mother's gentle words, also welcoming and caring. With her language, my mother offered me the gift to name that world and everything in it. She gave me a language that allowed me to make sense of the universe. My mother tongue endowed me with the magic of speaking the first word I ever spoke. My mother tongue gave me the power to name.

Deceptively simple words in that primordial language now have the force to elicit potent memories, to stir in me the most meaningful of evocations. A word in Spanish can bring back the aroma of freshly brewed coffee, the scent of my mother's breast, the sounds of *coquís* chanting in the night. A word in that original language can bring me back to a time I may have thought forgotten, but that exists in the brain, unerasable, enduring. These Spanish words have the power to contain within them all that I am. This is why I will always defend the rights of children to maintain the language of their mothers. I know that wiping out a mother tongue is the same as obliterating a universe.

This is the first time I've tried to reconstruct my mother's life, set down her spare biography, a task as daunting as it is laden with sorrow and regret for all that was lost. Her name was Isabel Oliveras Quijano. She was born in Caimito, a village near Arecibo on the northern coast of Puerto Rico. Her mother died when she was a child and she and her two sisters were brought up by Andrea Quijano, a maternal aunt. Her elder sister was a young adult when she died in a fire. My mother, the middle child, died at the age of eighteen or nineteen. Her younger sister married an older man. After the marriage, she turned into a *loca,* an elastic term in Puerto Rico that can mean anything from a homosexual male to a woman with fanciful ideas to a psychotic female. She was put away in a mental hospital where she died, it is rumored, by her own hand. The three sisters were too young to die, and having learned about this history of dead young women in my mother's family I was convinced for years that I, too, would experience an early death.

As so many people have done through the ages, my mother moved from the country to the city in search of work. She settled in El Fanguito, literally "the little mud," in San Juan. It was one of the worst shantytowns in Puerto Rico where cardboard and tar-paper shacks were propped up on stilts in a mud-filled swamp that collected the raw sewage of the city. When the tide was high and the winds lifted, the stench was unbearable. I know because as a teenager I often visited paternal relatives there before the shantytown was razed and the swamp filled to construct the first leg of Expresso Las Américas, an expressway that would run from San Juan to Río Piedras and has now expanded through most of the island.

My mother was a teenager probably sixteen or seventeen when she married my father and had me. On one of my trips to El Fanguito I met the midwife who delivered me. Appropriately, her name was Doña Luz. To give birth in Spanish is *dar a luz* or give to the light and I was given to the light in that shantytown shack buttocks first in what had to be an unbearably painful breech birth. I imagine that my mother's pain was like a bolt of lightning cleaving her in two while I swam the difficult waters to the shores of her thighs. Though we both could have died, my mother refused to be taken to the municipal hospital, convinced that people go to hospitals to die. At the time, this was probably true. Poor people went to the hospital when it was already too late.

My mother named me after the singer Alba Nydia Jusino. I have attempted to find recordings of my mother's favorite singer. Not finding them, I've had to make do with the voices and lyrics of other female singers of that era: Blanca Rosa Gil, Carmen Delia Dipiní, Virginia López, searching for my mother in the cadence of their songs, in the love-saturated words where she found solace.

Doña Luz remembered that my mother was wholly devoted to me and carried me everywhere. I was never out of her sight, she stressed. I imagine my teenage mother crossing the creaking board, slung over the mud, from her shack to the dirt road. I imagine her looking up at the haze in the sky and opening an umbrella as a shield against the punishing sun while I straddled her hip. After my birth there were no others and my mother succumbed like the banana plant that produces only one bunch and, after it has fruited, is cut down to the ground. I imagine how hard it must have been for her to die, to know that she would surrender me to a dubious fate. Did she face death with equanimity? Was someone with her at that moment when she crossed from her world of illness and poverty to the chasm of the unknown? Did she turn her parched lips to this person and whisper, "take care of *la nena*," not realizing that promises made to the dying are rarely kept? And where was I? I was always with her, according to Doña Luz, so did I witness her death? Did I, understanding my mother's deepest wish that someone take care of her *nena*, acquiesce to this request and become my own mother? For her sake?

Her love and devotion during those early years must have been so fierce that despite later disruptions they gave me the inner strength to become what she wanted me to be. For that is the intimate duty of women who lose their mothers young. We construct an ideal concept of what our mothers' aspirations for themselves and for us might have been and we set out, unwaveringly, to achieve them. We act on their behalf, to make their deaths make sense, to atone in our own way for the suffering and pain they endured. In Nicholasa Mohr's novel *Nilda* there is a moving scene at the deathbed of the young protagonist's mother. The mother urges her daughter to pursue her dreams because she never had the opportunity to achieve her own. Mohr, whose mother died when she was fourteen, later wrote in her splendid memoir, *Growing Up Inside the Sanctuary of My Imagination*: "My mother grieved that she was dying without ever having known herself. It was an empty feeling, a void deep inside her being. She made me promise that I would achieve my goals, no matter what. 'Please,' she implored, 'don't die like me.'" So it is that we, the motherless daughters of women who died with so many unrealized and shattered dreams, march forward in life with an irrevocable and solemn mission, to live our mothers' aspirations. By realizing their dreams, we become part of a whole, merging with them, as the Jamaican poet Lorna Goodison expresses so beautifully in "I Am Becoming My Mother": "Her birth waters sang like rivers / my mother is now me."

I often wonder about my mother's dreams. I know she worked as a seamstress in a blouse factory on Fernández Juncos Avenue in Santurce. She supported the aunt who had raised her and her aunt's son, a crippled man who was driven around the shantytown in a wooden wheelbarrow. After marrying her, and it is unclear why my father married her, he left. I heard a story once that illuminates the disharmony in which my mother lived. In El Fanguito she lived with a woman and her grown daughter who were both in love with my father. They loathed my mother because it was she whom he finally married. The women fought with her constantly until one day, during a particularly heated argument, they pushed her into the sewage. My mother was pregnant with me at the time. I've heard that she took a penny's worth of water bread and a bottle of Kola Champagne to work. This was her breakfast and lunch. Her immune system, weakened by pregnancy and malnutrition, would have been low. The sickening immersion in the filth of the swamp probably precipitated her illness. If she was married and pregnant, where was my father? Why wasn't he with her? Why was she living with strangers? Why didn't he protect her? Why wasn't he around when I was born? Why did he allow her to be buried in a potter's field?

A graffiti artist has smeared the word LUST in black spray paint on a brick wall near The Marine Society and I construct the only possible anagram: SLUT. Interesting. Lust is the one emotion that has effectively propelled my father. He and I were never close, though I am his image. He once told me that my face may be just like his, but my body is exactly like my mother's. I've since felt like a monster from ancient myths, a sphinx or a centaur or a griffin, a hybrid composed of dissimilar parts subsisting uneasily with each other. My father and I had a falling-out and he disappeared from my life for twenty-five years. Then he surfaced again, an old man looking for his eldest daughter, and wanting to know what had happened to her so he could die in peace. He marveled that I had come so far with neither mother nor father. That I had done it alone. We reconciled for a while and I visited him in Manatí, Puerto Rico, where he now lives. Our meetings were full of ambivalence and discomfort. But what finally drove me away from him, in a flurry of anger and despair, was his refusal to talk about my mother. What is it with him? I thought. The only thing I've ever asked of him, the only gift he could possibly give me is information about my mother, and this is the information he chooses to withhold? A refusal far worse than spitting in my face. What kind of a man denies his daughter this precious knowledge? Because I was brought up by his mother and surrounded by his family, I knew everything there was to know about him, and anything I may have missed he made certain to tell me after we reconciled.

His mother gave him away to relatives when he was small and he ended up homeless. He roamed from shack to shack in the mountains of Manatí scrounging for food, working at whatever he could find. He had to quit school after only a few months and go to work breaking rocks at a quarry for twelve to fourteen hours a day. People used to beat him just for the fun of it. When he was older, he'd line up at construction sites early in the morning with dozens of other workers hoping he'd be chosen to mix cement or carry buckets of gravel for the day. To improve his chances he'd show up with a toothpick stuck between his teeth so the foreman would think he had just had breakfast and was strong enough to work. He hadn't had anything to eat in days, he said, but those were the tricks he had to play to get by. He survived by foraging for wild berries, setting traps for birds and snakes and roasting them on kindling he collected. By the time he met and married my mother, he had moved to El Fanguito, learned to drive a truck, and was delivering milk. The dairy company accountant taught him rudimentary reading and arithmetic skills because to keep the job he had to know how to square the accounts at the end of each day: to calculate how many bottles of milk he sold, how many had broken, and what was left. He always told this part of his story with no small amount of pride.

During our brief rapprochement, all he did was tell me these stories of starvation and cruelty, apparently to justify his neglect and abandonment of me and his mistreatment of my mother. I insisted that he talk to me about her. Again and again, he refused. He offered the flimsiest excuses: all of that was in the past, it was too painful, and he didn't want to dwell on it (though he rehashed the stories of his childhood on countless occasions with an excruciating excess of detail). There was nothing to tell, he said. He loved my mother, married her, and she died—end of story. At last he made the admission I knew was behind his reluctance. He was afraid I would be angry with him if he told me what had happened. From what I've pieced together I can assume that my father married my mother so he could sleep with her. My father's promiscuity was legendary and, according to people who knew him well, there wasn't a woman he set his sights on who didn't succumb to his vaunted charms. My mother must have been a tough conquest, demanding and securing marriage before her surrender. I imagine that once he achieved his predatory pleasure, he lost interest and left her, most probably for a woman named Delia whom he had been romancing at the same time he was courting my mother. Without thinking about the consequences of his actions, without a thought for my mother, he left her pregnant with his child in a shack of hostile strangers. History has an irksome way of repeating itself. So it is not surprising that later he would abandon me too.

When my mother died, I was handed over to my paternal grandmother. The same woman who had abandoned my father and his siblings when he was a child became my guardian. Before that, I lived briefly with *titi* Andrea, who, having raised my mother, was willing to repeat the process with me, a course broken by my father's sudden appearance. My father's menopausal mother, living in the South Bronx with a younger husband, wanted the last chance life had afforded her to bring up a child. And I was available. So it was that my father, who had not seen me since he left my mother, showed up at the Arecibo village where I was living and took me away, on an airplane this time, far away from *titi* Andrea.

My grandmother despised her sons' wives. This disdain was not reserved for the living. It included *la difunta*, the deceased, as she called my mother. She called me *la huérfana*, the orphan. She objectified my mother and me and treated us as less than human. But I held on to whatever I possessed of my mother even when I was commanded to call my grandmother Mami, forcing me to negate the existence of my real mother, whose presence must have been very much alive in my mind. Compelled to call someone else Mami, forbidden from talking about my mother, I became adept at all things hidden. I turned into a silent child and learned to keep my feelings tucked away in a deep recess where no one could violate them. In this way, I lost my mother again.

Having lost my mother, I've gone through life with the pain of an amputated limb. The pain of a limb that has been sawn off, but that remains in the severed nerve, in the scar tissue. A phantom pain. While my mother lived she held me down in a secure place where I could never float away and disappear. After she died, I was adrift and a familiar unreality settled in me. Rather than providing stability, life with my grandmother was charged with further stresses of separation. She had her own phantoms to deal with, the emotional burdens of her disturbing background, her losses, her struggle to live each day without much hope for the future. Often, when life became too perilous, she would pick up her cardboard suitcase and board a plane back to Puerto Rico. I can't remember the many places I lived in as a child. I vaguely recall some of the people in those foster homes, my grandmother disappearing and reappearing, and I remember waiting, in that desperate way daughters have, for my father to somehow find it in his heart to love me. Altered irrevocably by death and having experienced so many upheavals, my life seemed illusory and I always felt out of place. Virginia Woolf, whose mother died when she was thirteen, expresses precisely this sense of alienation when in her novel *Mrs. Dalloway* the protagonist feels as though she "sliced like a knife through everything; at the same time outside, looking on. She had a perpetual sense of being out, far out to sea and alone."

The sense of disconnection and difference we motherless women feel throughout our lives is understandable, having had no mirrors to reflect ourselves as we would become. I had no one to guide me into womanhood, no one to validate my efforts, to reassure me that my dreams and aspirations were not far-fetched, that I had the right to seek fulfillment and joy. It's no coincidence, I suppose, that I became obsessed with doing things right. Getting good grades was imperative, gaining my teachers' respect essential. Without this outsider's validation, I knew I would die.

I've always felt that I've lived two parallel lives, like the I rails on a railroad track. One is the life I have lived since my mother died. The other is the life I would have lived if she were here. As I perform the routine tasks of daily living, I can't help thinking that if my mother lived, I could be standing at the supermarket checkout counter chatting idly with her about the August heat or sharing the latest gossip. I could be calling her on the phone to ask her advice on how to deal with one of her grandchildren. I imagine that if she were alive, instead of having a quick sandwich while I edited a manuscript, I'd be dropping by to see how she was and she'd have a nice *asopao de camarones* prepared because she knew I would come and shrimp stew is my favorite.

After a lifetime of living in places where I've been a stranger, I now feel that these parallel lives have miraculously converged into a third life. A life of acceptance of my mother's death and reconciliation with the two lives I've lived because of her loss. I know I have clung to the pain of my mother's death because that pain is all that connects me to her. And I've come to the realization that it's not necessary to let the pain go. There is a space in my heart for the pain and nostalgia of what has been lost. But the pain need not destroy me as it destroyed my mother. I can find a safe place for it, a space where my mother will always be, and let the ache of her loss settle there, undisturbed. I can now, in this third life, rekindle a relationship with my partner without the expectation of being mothered and at the same time wanting to mother. I can live without the constant fear that the people I love will disappear, without the belief that unless I'm perfect I'm not worthy of being loved. Though I still feel the urge to tell the people I meet, "My mother died when I was two," and expect that phrase to define me, though I still feel fundamentally different from women with mothers, I can now live with the knowledge that peace is possible because at the end of the line my two parallel lives have come together.

At Richmond Station, I hasten to the street. It's rush hour, and people come and go driven by the daily grind. I move away from the bustle and make my way to the park. I close my eyes and shut out the noise of cars and voices. A slight breeze lifts the branches of a tree and I feel my mother's kiss on my cheek, her lips worn smooth by lullabies. I am sitting in the ocean of her lap, squinting under the tropical sun, taking in the warm, salty scent of her arm. Humidity dapples her bare breast. I revel in her aroma of sand and palm fronds and milk. As I taste my mother's body I envision the cord that binds us together and understand, finally, her gift. She gave me a never-ending fountain of love that would sustain me throughout the journey I had to undertake without her. Her love made me strong, determined, and capable. My mother's love gave me the essential integrity of my life.

Dolores Montañez Thomas, Piri Thomas's mother

*"When it came to courage and putting her life on the line,
Mami would not hesitate for a second."*

Piri Thomas is the author of the classic memoir Down These Mean Streets *(Vintage) as well as three other volumes,* Savior, Savior Hold My Hand *(Doubleday),* Seven Long Times *(Arte Público Press), and* Stories from El Barrio *(Knopf).*

Mami, a.k.a. Doña Lola

Mami, a.k.a. Dolores Montañez, a.k.a. Doña Lola, was born in 1911 in the hills of Cerro Gordo, above the town of Bayamón in Puerto Rico. Mami was the youngest of six surviving children from a family of fourteen. Mami said some of them had died at birth and germs killed the others while they were still babies. When their mami and popi died in an accident Mami and her siblings became orphans. Since Mami was the youngest and could not fend for herself, she was farmed out to live with other people as "*una criada*," which meant that in some places she was accepted as family while in other places she was treated like a servant.

During her teens, Mami learned to sew and got a job doing piecework in a dress factory. She found a decent place to live and was able to support herself. When she was sixteen her eldest sister, Catín, invited her to visit her in Nueva Yawk, with the idea that if Mami liked Nueva Yawk, she would help her find a job in the garment district, and then Mami could stay with her and help out with the rent or find a place of her own. For the previous five years, Catín had been living in Nueva Yawk's East Harlem, on 110th Street between Madison and Park Avenues. She was single at the time but a very nice man was interested in her.

In 1926 Mami arrived in Nueva Yawk aboard the SS *Marine Tiger*, which had been bringing Puerto Ricans to the United States ever since it had been retired as a WWI troop carrier. Tía Catín and a few friends were at the dock to meet the ship— among them a handsome young man who had been born in Cuba. Like Mami and Catín, he was an orphan himself, due to the yellow-fever epidemic, which had orphaned hundreds if not thousands of Cuban children. His name was Juan Tomás a.k.a. Johnny. He had come to Nueva Yawk via Puerto Rico pretending to be Puerto Rican, since they had become U.S. citizens by an act of Congress in 1917 and Cubans were aliens. When Mami got off the *Marine Tiger* there were many hugs all around. Catín introduced Mami to Popi-to-be and there was no doubt that for Juan Tomás it was love at first sight. Mami hid her feelings but her smile told Catín that she found Juan Tomás quite interesting, a gallant man who had bowed and kissed her hand at being introduced. I guess it was Juan Tomás's old-world charm that impressed her.

The following Saturday evening Catín threw a dinner party and invited more friends to celebrate her sister's first trip to Nueva Yawk. Among those invited was Juan Tomás, resplendent in a dark cream suit, a light cream shirt, tie, shoes, and spats to match. Mami was wearing a beautiful white dress with ruffles that matched her soft white leather shoes.

The two-bedroom apartment was filled with the aroma of Puerto Rican cuisine and the sensuous sounds of a bolero. Johnny Tomás nodded toward Mami and then to those dancing and, with a smile, Mami came into his arms and together they were sensational. *Bueno*, to get to the point, eighteen months later they were married. Exactly nine months later, I was born, on September 30, 1928, thus keeping gossip about a too-early birth from spreading through *los barrios* of Nueva Yawk, as well as up in the hills of Cerro Gordo.

By the time I was seven years old, in 1935, there were three children. My sister Lillian was five years old and my brother Ramón was three. The very great depression that came down on the world in 1929 was still weighing heavily on all poor people of the world, East Harlem being no exception. The welfare lines were long. People with hungry children to feed waited as patiently as possible. Many parents ate less so that their children could eat more. There was more work for women than for men, but for less pay. Popi spent long hours searching for work wherever he thought there might be a chance to be hired, but countless other men had the same idea, and in those days, as in these days, blacks and browns were the last to be hired and the first to be fired. Because she was a seamstress and a whiz on the sewing machine, Mami got a job working long hours for low wages, which was better than nothing—which was what Popi was earning. Here and there he found odd jobs at the docks, where men were hired to do the work of horses for wages that were only a little higher than what the women earned. Popi hated to be on home relief, so with what both he and Mami earned, we stayed off welfare as long as we could. I had a shoe-shine box and I shined shoes on the corner of 103rd Street and Lexington Avenue, a spot I had to fight for every time I set up. I also did my bit to help the family by hanging around the home-relief food

depot where handouts were given to the poor. I waited for someone who was sick and tired of canned corned beef to dump the
cans into the empty lot on the corner. I had to fight to snatch as
many cans as I could since I wasn't the only kid with the same
idea. We took them to Joe's Pet Shop, where Joe would give us a
pigeon for every three cans of beef. On a good day, I could grab
enough cans to bring home three pigeons and we would have
pigeon soup, fried pigeon, pigeon with rice and beans, or pigeon
with whatever.

Mami brought extra work home and her old sewing machine
roared into the early morning light and then, with only a couple
of hours' rest, she got up and went back to work at the clothing
factory. Popi tried to save money on the electric bill by inserting
el pillo, "the thief"—a piece of insulated wire that was bare at
each end—into the electric box to keep the amount of current
registered down to a minimum, which added up to a nice savings
at the end of the month. Mami, being a good Christian, was
against Popi using el pillo because it was not honest according to
God; but according to Popi, it was all right for poor people to use
it. So when Mami wasn't looking, Popi would slip the piece of
twisted wire into the fuse box, referring to it as "the good thief,"
because, after all, wasn't the electric company rich enough as
it was?

Mami was one of the great mommies of El Barrio in Nueva
Yawk. And, like many other moms, she was generous to a fault.
She was loved and respected by Puerto Ricans and non–Puerto
Ricans alike. She always cooked extra food just in case somebody dropped in. Mami knew without a doubt if they were hungry. If there was not enough food, Mami brought out the little
libreta, "the notebook," and one of us went down to La Bodega,
purchased some food, and the debt would be recorded on its
pages. In no time at all something delicious would be steaming

in our pot. Many were the *familias* that thanked God for the bodega and the *libreta*, which allowed them credit up to a certain amount, whereas no supermarket would ever think of trusting them, not even for a single dime.

When it came to courage and putting her life on the line, Mami would not hesitate for a second. One day, at about five-thirty in the afternoon, she had to deliver some work to the garment factory. She told us she'd be back in an hour or so and that we were not to open the door to strangers or to open any windows or at any time to play with sharp knives or matches. My sister Lillian, my brother Ramón, and I promised Mami by solemnly crossing our hearts and hoping to die. She hugged and kissed each of us, lifted her large bundle of finished skirts to her small shoulder and told us it was quite possible that Popi, who was looking for work in New Jersey, might get home even before she did. She said that we could listen to the radio and that if we got hungry there were milk and cookies to hold us until she came home and made dinner. Struggling under her burden, Mami closed the door and firmly locked the three locks behind her. Through the closed door she called back, "*Por favor*, don't forget what I told you, children." "Don't worry, Mami," I yelled back. "We won't forget."

We listened to Mami's footsteps as they made their way down three flights of stairs; we strained our ears trying to follow her steps all the way to the street. It would have been nicer to have lived facing the street instead of the backyard. There would have been more to see.

I turned on the radio and tuned in to a Spanish station, brought out playing cards, the domino game, some old magazines and comic books, put them all on top of the coffee table, and let each of the kids choose. Since they couldn't read, they could at least look at the pictures. I wondered who would get home first, Mami or Popi, not that we were nervous about being all alone, but after all, we were kids trying hard to act grown-up. After an hour without Mami or Popi returning, I put us all to making peanut-butter sandwiches so that we wouldn't get nervous. With the sandwiches and glasses of milk, we all felt better—until Lillian smelled smoke. We stared apprehensively at each other before I blurted out, "We didn't light any matches 'cause we didn't cook anything. We just made some peanut-butter sandwiches. Who needs matches for that?"

Lillian and Ramón nodded in unison and the three of us walked throughout the four-room apartment, sniffing up and down and all around, but not finding a trace of smoke or even an itty-bitty lick of fire. Lillian's eyes went to the fire escape window. She looked up and began howling like a fire-engine siren. She had spotted thick swirls of black smoke pouring out of the back apartment two floors above us. Ramón followed Lillian's eyes and joined the chorus, wailing even louder. "Quiet, you guys, somebody's just burning bacon, so take it easy, okay? I'll get a chair and we can open the top lock and get the heck out of here."

Around that time, Mami was walking home from the garment factory, and as she turned onto our block, she saw a crowd of people. More people were running out of our old tenement and clouds of black smoke were billowing from the roof. She fought her way against the down current of people, who were all in a mad dash to get out to the streets. Mami made her way to our floor, where we were having a hard time getting the top lock open. I must have really messed it up and jammed it when I hit the lock with the hammer while trying to get the darn thing to open up. We were trapped, our goose was cooked! We couldn't get out through the fire escape because the windows were barred and locked and we didn't have the keys. When we heard Mami screaming through the door for us to open the locks, we felt as if the Savior had arrived! We screamed back that the top lock was stuck and would not unlock. Mami tried with her keys again, but to no avail. I thought I should have never smacked that lock with Popi's heavy hammer. I felt like blaming some of it on my sister and brother, but they were innocent as only really little kids can be.

"Don't get excited, *niños*, just keep calm and everything is going to be okay. God is going to help us," Mami's voice assured us. She began banging on the door of the next apartment. "Doña Josefa, Doña Josefa," Mami called out, "*por favor*, open the door. In case you don't know it, there is a fire on the fifth floor but it will get down here to the third floor before long. *Por favor, abra la puerta, señora, señora,* I need to use your fire escape to get my children out or they will burn up!" Mami beat harder on the old lady's door and I also began to beat on the wall that we shared with Doña Josefa's apartment with my fists and was immediately joined by the little fists of my frightened siblings. We heard Doña Josefa answer in a sleepy voice as her door opened and Mami, at the top of her voice, repeated her warning about the fire on the top floor, and would she *please* let Mami use her fire escape so she could rescue her children.

We heard Mami run into Doña Josefa's apartment without waiting for permission and she headed for the back fire escape. We followed the sound of her running footsteps and headed in the same direction. Mami climbed out on the fire escape and came to our side. We watched through the window as she tested the bars to see if they could be opened. But without the key, the only way to open the gate was to break the huge locks. Meanwhile, the air was getting thicker with smoke as the fire ate its way down. Mami checked out the window ledge that led to the bathroom. To get there, she would have to climb over the railing of the fire escape and then place one foot precariously on the windowsill. After establishing a fingerhold, she would need to pull her other foot to the sill and then somehow open or break the window in order to get into the apartment. We watched Mami gauge the distance from the fire escape to the bathroom sill. She then looked down at the three-story drop to the concrete backyard, which I knew was filled with boxes and trash, discarded bottles and pipes. Mami looked up at the sky that was darkening with smoke and listened to the loud wails coming from the street. Then she stood on the fire escape at our window, smiled at us, and made like she was hugging us. With a silent prayer she turned and climbed over the fire escape railing. Holding on tightly with her left hand, she found finger grips on the bathroom window jamb and brought over her right foot. She then adjusted her grip and pulled the rest of her body over to the sill with a strong, careful heave. I prayed to God that Mami would hold on to the ledge and not fall to her death amid the junk on that hard concrete. The smoke was making Mami cough a little. She pushed down on the top window and it worked perfectly, rolling down smoothly. Without a moment's hesitation, she climbed into the bathroom, a little bit scratched but safe and sound, and we all hugged each other, coughing.

Mami said, "Vámonos, muchachos. Let's get out of here before the fire gets any closer. The smoke is getting a little thick." She herded us to the front door, where she checked out that the dead bolt on the top lock had been jammed. She turned it and the door opened to our cheers. We all ran into the hall just in time to meet the firemen rushing up the stairs to fight the blaze on the floors above. One big fireman guided us down to the street to an ambulance, where we were examined for smoke inhalation and injuries. We were found to be fine, and released. As we joined our many neighbors on the sidelines who were gaping at the firemen's progress, word spread that the fire had been put out, and a huge roar went up. All that was needed was time to be sure there were no remaining hot spots and that the air had cleared inside. Then we could all go back to our apartments safely.

It was my sister Lillian who caught sight of Popi coming down the block, looking harried as he searched desperately for the somebodies who were us. I could see the relief on his face when we all rushed into his arms. "Thank God," he moaned. "I was afraid that something terrible had happened to you." Mami came into Popi's arms, too, saying, "You don't need to worry. Me and the children took care of everything okey-dokey." Popi hugged Mami really hard and kissed her even harder. We kids just hung onto him and told him what a hero our mami had been. Lillian told him how Mami had climbed over the fire escape and crawled in through the toilet window to save our lives. Even Ramón added his two cents' worth. Popi suggested that we go to Tía Catín's apartment where we all could take a shower and wash our clothes. We could tell Mami's sister all about our great adventure and our heroic mami. Mami smiled and said not to forget what great heroes we children had been, too. Popi said we could buy some fried chicken and a quart of strawberry ice cream. After washing up, with Catín we could think of something else nice to do.

"Just being together would be the nicest thing in the world," Mami smiled.

"I second that," Popi grinned and swung Ramón up on his shoulders. Mami took Lillian by the hand and I took Mami's other hand and gave it a squeeze. Mami squeezed back and I knew that everything in our world was okay again. After all, with Mami for a mother and she married to my great pops, being together as a family was the best thing in the world!

Punto!

Gustavo Pérez Firmat in his mother's arms, Havana, 1949

*"Mother was the strongest person he knew,
but also the most vulnerable."*

～ ～ ～ ～ ～ GUSTAVO PÉREZ FIRMAT

Gustavo Pérez Firmat was born in Havana, Cuba, and raised in Miami, Florida. A recipient of fellowships from the National Endowment for the Humanities, the American Council of Learned Societies, and the Guggenheim Foundation, he is currently David Feinson Professor of Humanities at Columbia University. His numerous volumes of literary and cultural criticism include Literature and Liminality *and* Do the Americas Have a Common Literature? *(both Duke University Press) and* Life on the Hyphen: The Cuban-American Way *(University of Texas Press), which was awarded the Eugene M. Kayden University Press National Book Award. His collections of poetry in Spanish and English include* Carolina Cuba, Equivocaciones, *and* Bilingual Blues. *His most recent books are* Cincuenta lecciones de exilio y desexilio *(Ediciones Universal) and the novel* Anything but Love *(Arte Público). Like Frank in the story that follows, Gustavo Francisco Pérez Firmat is also the author of a memoir,* Next Year in Cuba: A Cubano's Coming of Age in America *(Anchor Books).*

Mami's Boy

They were in the middle of dinner when the phone rang; it was his father. "Your mother had another nightmare about you." He put her on the phone.

"So what did I do this time, Mami? Burn the house?"

"You gave me another *disgusto*."

Listening to his mother's dream—unlike his sketchy recollections, her dreams were always amazingly detailed—Frank didn't care what this particular *disgusto* was, only that it was another one, an imaginary sequel to the real-life nightmare he had already inflicted on her.

For his mother all the grief, all the tragedies of this world, all the myriad deliberate or inadvertent things that people do to hurt or harass one another, all the illnesses and misfortunes that befall us in the course of living—all this came down to one word, *disgusto*. It's difficult to find a translation for this word, which names an emotion without a precise English equivalent. "Disgust" won't do, because it suggests a visceral repulsion absent from the Spanish cognate; although someone who experiences disgust could also feel *disgustado*, it's quite possible to experience *disgusto* without being at all disgusted. Terms like "heartache" or "disappointment" hit closer to the mark, because, like them, *disgusto* conveys a deeply felt sense of private injury. Regardless of the circumstances, *disgustos* are always personal; the cause could be a typhoon, a typhus epidemic, or the stock-market crash—no matter. It's still an individual affront, an attack on an individual's right to peace and quiet, a *disgusto*.

What Frank had done to provoke his mother's *disgusto*, two years earlier, was to write a book. Oh, he had written books before, several of them, textbooks that taught American young people to ask for directions and order dinner in Spanish. These books had colorful covers and snappy titles like *¿Qué pasa? ¿Qué tal? ¿Qué se cuenta?* and *¿Y qué?* His mother proudly displayed them in her living room alongside her set of Lladró shepherds. But this book was different. The cover showed a grainy black-and-white photo of Frank when he was six or seven years old, standing on a Havana street corner next to his parents. Inside was the story of his family.

When his mother found out that Frank was writing a book about them, she said to him, "I hope you are going to treat us kindly in this book because I watch those TV talk shows and the parents always get blamed for everything."

He assured her, without completely believing it, that the book would make no embarrassing revelations about anybody except himself. He told her that what he wanted was to understand, not blame; but he knew even then, before he had written more than a few paragraphs, that some of his theories were bound to upset her. His mother tended to have one five-letter explanation for most things: F-I-D-E-L. He agreed with her much of the time, but there were things not even the Cuban Revolution could account for. His mother always complained that, in exile, her life had been an endless string of *disgustos*. He wanted to understand why, even if his explanations struck his mother as too psychological. She had a word for psychology, too: *bobería*, "nonsense."

He finished the memoir in a few months because he had been writing it in his head and his heart for twenty years. When he received the first copies from the publisher, he FedExed one to his mother in Miami, then took off for the beach with his daughter. A week later, tanned and rested and somewhat apprehensive, he called her.

"How could you write this about us, Yunior?" She was on the verge of tears. Since he shared his father's first name, his mother always called him by this nickname, which he disliked but accepted. "What are people going to think about us, about your father?"

She was distraught that he had written about their early years in exile—tough, penurious times when he and his brothers took turns sleeping on the floor of the living room because their parents could not afford a large enough house. For the kids, sleeping three to a room had been a blast; it was like camping out indoors night after night. But for his parents seeing their children lying on the floor had been a real hardship. In his book Frank described his mother picking up the sheets and blankets every morning, folding them and tucking them away under the cushions of the sofa. Back in Cuba she had owned a big house with enough rooms for all her children and enough servants to pick up after them. He wanted to show the contrast, to dramatize how much she had lost; but that's not how his mother saw it. "When my friends read this, my face is going to fall off from shame," she said.

Then she spent a long time—at least that's how it seemed to him—enumerating all the mistakes in his book. He had forgotten to mention some relatives (it's true, he had), erred about dates (guilty as charged), and confused some incidents from his childhood with his brother Pepe's (yes, that too). But the worst thing he had done, in addition to writing about sleeping on the floor, was to reveal that for a short while his father had received U.S. government aid. His mother swore that it never happened, they had never taken *un kilo* from *los americanos*; and yet Frank was sure that he remembered seeing the perforated green checks on the kitchen counter.

After his mother had finished her list of mistakes, she threatened to write her own memoir in order to set the family record straight. "Then you and I can go on *Oprah* and scream at each other, like the Americans."

Frank was dismayed by how starkly the book he had written differed from the book his mother had read. Where he had written sorrow, she had read resentment. Where he had written love, she had read spite. Where he had written hope, she had read abandonment. To him, the book was an act of homage; to her, a humiliation.

When she finally hung up the phone, he sat down and made a list of all of his inaccuracies, as best as he could remember them, hoping that he could correct them someday. If his mother wrote her version, as she threatened to do, would it be as difficult for her to write about him as it had been for him to write about her? Of all the chapters in the book, the one about his mother had given him the most trouble, because she was more of an enigma than anyone else in his family. His father he could understand. To understand his father all he had to do was to look at himself. His brothers he understood also, because when he looked at them he saw pieces of his own personality. He had found it easy to write about fathers and sons, uncles and nephews, brothers; but writing about his mother was something else altogether. The more he thought about her, the more intractable she seemed, like a mystery without a solution.

And yet it was she who had gotten him into the habit of jotting down thoughts and memories. His father was an active, practical man who, as far as Frank knew, had never written a sentence in his life. But as long as he could remember, his mother was always writing something—letters to friends, notes to herself, recipes for the cook, lists of chores for the maids. One of her proudest possessions was an ever-expanding shelf of care-fully annotated photo albums in which she recorded the places, dates, and guest lists of all of the family births, baptisms, gradua-tions, weddings, and funerals. Dedicating a different set of albums to each of her three boys, she always wrote her notes addressing the son in question, no matter how old he was at the time of the event. Frank's wedding album began: "You were mar-ried on August 12th, 1975, at 7:35 in the evening, in the Church of the Little Flower in Coral Gables, Florida. Father Jef-frey Vaughn officiated at your wedding."

"Memory is tragic," she used to reply when asked why she kept such painstaking records. "But if I write things down, they will stay true for you and your children and grandchildren." Because his mother's albums had been Frank's source for much of the information in his book, he even had thought of her as his silent collaborator, his coauthor, as responsible for his life story as she had been for his life.

Kind but irascible, tender but stern, Frank's mother was the strongest person he knew but also the most vulnerable. Her strength and her weakness was her family. It seemed to Frank that she never thought in the first person. Whenever she told stories, which she often did, the subject of all her sentences was *nosotros,* "we." Whatever affected her as an individual, whatever unfulfilled longings or secret regrets she may have had in her long life, didn't seem to matter to her. At least she never talked about them. When she was a child, her siblings called her Mami Chiquita because even then she had made it her mission to hold her family together.

An episode that, for Frank, epitomized his mother: When his daughter Emily was still in preschool, Frank's mother got a letter from her youngest brother, whom she had not seen since she had left Cuba. Initially a supporter of the Revolution, he had stayed behind on the island. When he finally left, ill and embittered, he settled in New York where he lived for years without any contact with the family. Then one day he wrote to his sister, his Mami Chiquita, to say that he was dying and wanted to spend his last months in Miami. Frank remembered his mother reading the letter and crying, then sitting down at the dining room table to write a reply to her brother. With her granddaughter Emily draped all over her, Frank's mother composed a long letter to her brother, offering her house and money for the trip. That was his mother: the bridge between generations, the glue that sealed the family's cracks.

He remembered other things about his mother: chocolate milk in Mason jars . . . the gold-leafed missal, bulging with holy cards . . . summer afternoons of canasta under an umbrella at the beach . . . leaving school early to watch a double feature of American movies . . . checking under the seats at the movie theater for bombs . . . crying on the way to school because he didn't want to be separated from her.

And then he recalled something that he had been determined to forget, an incident that he promised himself he would never write or speak about. He wasn't even sure what to call it— a fight, a misunderstanding, a nightmare, another *disgusto*. Anytime he thought about his mother, this one unnamable thing haunted him; when he sensed that it was sneaking into his consciousness, he willed it away. It was the kind of memory that made him turn up the volume on the TV set or break out singing just to drown out the screaming in his head. Perhaps one of the reasons that he found it so difficult to write about his mother was that he felt compelled to skirt this incident. Like a boulder in the road, it wouldn't let him through, and he didn't have the strength to move it.

It had happened the Christmas after his second divorce. All

divorces are messy, but bicultural ones can be especially difficult, because sometimes the sense of betrayal poisons your attitude toward a whole culture. Fortunately, Frank's second marriage had been brief and produced no children. Still, the bitterness remained—for Frank because he couldn't believe that he had been dumped by an *americana;* for Emily, because her life had been shattered a second time; and for Frank's mother, because she was convinced that her son, having bailed out on his first marriage, had not done enough to make his second marriage work. Of her three sons, Frank was the only one to have divorced—and twice! When Frank left his first wife, his mother penciled in the margin of his wedding album, after the sentence indicating the date of the marriage, *la primera vez,* "for the first time." Now she had had to revise the entries for the second marriage as well. As always, she blamed Fidel.

Her custom was to celebrate Nochebuena in her house in Miami with those of her children and grandchildren who could attend. Year after year she had refused Frank's invitation to spend Christmas in North Carolina with him, but now that he was living alone and didn't visit Miami as often as he used to, she wanted to show solidarity with her son and her granddaughter. If he couldn't join the family for Christmas, she would bring the family to him.

Frank's father refused to fly because he was afraid that the plane would be hijacked to Cuba, so his parents took the long train ride to Raleigh. They arrived in time for his father's birthday, December 17, which also happened to be the birthday of the woman Frank had been dating. His mother wasn't thrilled that he was involved with Debbie, another American. Frank's first wife, a *cubana,* had not remarried, and his mother hadn't given up hope that Frank would eventually get over his infatuation with *americanas* and go back to his own kind.

The first few days of the visit were awkward but peaceful. The deer bounding across the backyard and a granddaughter of grade-school age were enough to keep his mother cheerful and busy. His father, who was more difficult to entertain, read the papers, watched game shows, and explored the neighborhood. Frank gave his parents his bedroom, which had the only queen-sized bed in the house, so that they would have more privacy. He slept on the sofa in the living room, as he had done when he was a teenager.

On the morning of Nochebuena, his parents borrowed the car and took Emily to the mall for some last-minute shopping. By the time they returned, Debbie had arrived to help with the preparations for that night's dinner. Frank's mother had agreed to cook a well-seasoned leg of pork, her specialty, while Debbie was contributing a turkey with dressing and cranberry sauce. Debbie's sisters were going to chip in with wine and desserts.

After wrapping the gifts, his mother went into the bedroom. Half an hour later, she was still there. Frank knocked on the door, asking if anything were wrong.

"We're fine Yunior," his mother said in English. He could tell that she wasn't. He knocked again.

His father opened the door. He was wearing the blue parka he had bought for the visit. He looked odd. This thin man who never wore anything but guayaberas was buried inside bubbles of padding and fabric. His mother was lying on the bed, reading a biography of Napoleon she had bought at the mall. She glanced up from the book, "Yes?"

"Are you okay, Ma?" That's what he called her when he spoke to her in English. A small revenge for all the years she had called him "Yunior."

She sighed. "How can I be okay when I see what is happening to my granddaughter?"

"What are you talking about, Ma?"

"The example you are giving her."

"Example of what?"

"You and your brothers never saw anything like this at our house."

"I don't know what you're talking about."

"You and your new friend."

That morning, during the outing with her grandparents, Emily had mentioned that "Papi's girlfriend" sometimes spent the night at their house.

"This has nothing to do with Emily," he said, knowing that he was wrong. "Besides, Debbie's my fiancée."

"It shows a lack of respect for your daughter. Not to mention Marta."

Marta's continuing intimacy with his mother was a sore point with Frank, and he tried not to bring up the subject. It had been seven years since he left his first wife, but his mother talked about them as if he and Marta were still married.

"Keep Marta out of this," he said.

"Then think about your daughter. You want her to grow up to behave like that?"

"Like what?"

His mother was silent for a moment. She closed the book and placed it on her lap. "Like a *puta*."

He couldn't believe that his mother had just called Debbie a whore. Debbie was the woman he was in love with, the woman he planned to marry someday, the woman who at that very moment was downstairs baking brownies with Emily. "You're wrong," he blurted out, not knowing what else to reply. "Debbie's not a *puta*."

His mother sprang up from the bed. In her sixties, she was still nimble enough to go bike-riding with her grandchildren.

He realized that she was furious. He knew and feared these bursts of anger. One moment she was the softest, kindest person in the world; the next, she could rip your heart out.

"Let me tell you something else," she said, raising her voice. "You still have a few lessons to learn from your father about being a man."

An unlit cigar in his hand, his father was looking through the window at the house across the street. His long-standing policy was to stay out of all arguments between his wife and their sons. But he finally said, "I didn't raise you to behave this way, Frank."

Frank knew that his father hadn't raised him; his father had watched him grow. But he had stopped arguing about that a long time ago. It was another of the bargains he had struck with himself to avoid *disgustos*. So he said nothing.

His mother's voice turned soft again. "I look at you and I can tell you're not happy, Yunior. How could you be? You know this is immoral. No decent woman acts this way. If you were a *caballero*, you would tell her to sleep in her own home where she belongs."

The Spanish word for home is *hogar*, literally "hearth." For Frank it was the warmest, most beautiful word in the language.

"I don't want to get into this," he said, remembering other squabbles. "It's my life."

"You can say what you want. In our country the name for that kind of woman is *puta*."

That's when it happened. He felt a rush of rage and closed his eyes. He didn't know where all that anger came from, he didn't want to know. Eyes still closed, he swung wildly. When he opened them, he saw his mother sitting on the edge of the bed, holding the side of her face. His father lurched toward him and Frank swung again. He felt his fist dig into the cottony billows of the winter coat. Then he ran out of the room. Downstairs Emily and Debbie were decorating the brownies with M&Ms.

That evening Frank's parents met Debbie's sisters and her two teenaged children. Frank made sure that when he introduced the live-in boyfriend of Debbie's younger sister, he called him her *esposo*. But not a word was said about what had transpired that afternoon. After the meal, the Guerra-O'Neal families exchanged presents. Debbie spent the night with Frank on the sofa.

On Christmas morning Frank's mother and father took the train back to Florida. At the Amtrak station, as she said goodbye to her eldest son, Frank's mother whispered into his ear, "*Que Dios te ilumine*"—"May God enlighten you."

The night when Frank's father called him about his mother's nightmare, Frank had been working on an exercise about Spanish terms of endearment: *mi amor* (my love), *mi vida* (my life), *mi alma* (my soul), *mi corazón* (my heart). Ten years had passed, and he was still married to Debbie, with whom he'd had another daughter (they named her Carmen Ana in honor of his mother). In all this time neither he nor his parents had ever mentioned the punching incident. But each time he called his mother, which he did every Sunday evening, he had the feeling that her lively small talk was a way of covering up what was really on her mind.

Throughout the years Frank had tried, in small unobtrusive ways, to make up to her for what he had done; but he wasn't sure whether she recognized or appreciated his gestures, since she didn't acknowledge them. It seemed to him that his mother no longer treated him with the same tenderness, though he couldn't have said exactly why he felt this way. Sometimes he believed that if the incident ever did come up, his mother would deny that it took place.

When he hung up the phone, after reassuring her that Carmen Ana was fine (the nightmare had been about her), Frank went into his study and decided once and for all to write down his memories of the worst Christmas of his life. He needed to get them off his chest. He wanted to apologize, to atone, to let his mother know that the shame had never left him. But after typing a few sentences, he stopped. He was afraid that his mother would misunderstand his purpose, and that, instead of making things better between them, by writing about that day he would just be giving her one more *disgusto*.

F*eeling more than ever like Mami's boy, he erased the words from the screen.*

Liz Balmaseda with her mami, Ada Mas Balmaseda, aboard
the SS *Sovereign of the Seas,* December 1996

*Ada had been diagnosed with breast cancer metastasized to
the lung six months before and had just begun chemotherapy. "In a
casino, Mami's in another world, bless her soul."*

⟨ ⟨ ⟨ ⟨ ⟨ ⟨ ⟨ ⟨ ⟨ LIZ BALMASEDA

Liz Balmaseda is a Pulitzer Prize–winning columnist with the Miami Herald. She is the author, with Pedro José Greer, of Waking Up in America: How One Doctor Brings Hope to Those Who Need It *(Simon and Schuster). She is currently at work on a screenplay with singer Gloria Estefan.*

Travels with Mami

She is turning the last silvery token between her fingers, caressing it first on one side, then the other, as if to coax its hiding genie. She appears to be entranced, suspended in the dazzle of blinking neon, the little spinning fruit, spinning sevens, temperamental diamonds, blazing fireballs. Which one? Which one will get her last dollar? I can tell she's looking for the Wild Rose slots, the kind that came through for her in Reno, delivering three robust, pink roses, one next to the other, cha-cha-cha, and a sweet cascade of a thousand quarters.

But there are no rose machines in this casino. She eyes the progressives, but, nah, she'd have to play three coins to win the jackpot. So she heads for the trusty old black-and-white sevens.

With an air of ceremony, she rolls the token into the coin slot, inhales the casino's smoky vapors, and pulls the lever, setting off a grayish blur and then, finally, a skid of mismatched doo-dads.

Nada.

She takes a foil-wrapped hand-wipe from her fanny pack and rubs the coin smudges from her fingers.

Vamos.

Well, it's about time, I mutter to myself, my thin tolerance for this Barnum scene having reached a breaking point hours earlier. I've been trying to leave this casino for two hours. Hell, I've been trying to leave Nevada for two days. From the wistful last looks she is bestowing on this, the last casino in Wendover, the last, pit-stop town in northeastern Nevada, arid and color-less except for its noisy slots, you'd think we were leaving Cuba all over again. *Adiós, Tropicana,* her misty eyes seem to be say-ing. (Of course she doesn't mean the starry-roofed Havana cabaret, but the hotel in Vegas, where she pulled a lucky lever and won us a couple of tickets to that night's showgirl revue.)

Poor Mami. She's tried every delay tactic she can think of:

"Ay, I have to go the bathroom again."

"*Oye,* aren't you hungry?"

"*Mira,* the buffet is only four ninety-five. We can wait in line over here, by the slot tournament, *tú no crees?*"

But she knows it's over. Now, stoic, casino-free Utah awaits. We are nearly two-thirds of the way around our cross-country loop. This is Day Seventeen, which means we still have to drive through Utah, Colorado, Kansas, Missouri, Indiana, Kentucky, Tennessee, Georgia, and Florida before we get back home, to Miami.

～ ～ ～

The reason we are driving cross-country is because my mother doesn't fly—not on airplanes, at least. And, if by any freak chance she agreed to take a Vegas-bound flight one day, she couldn't pay me enough to get on that plane with her. What, are you nuts? There's not enough Xanax in all of Miami. So we take trains and buses. And we drive, barreling across generic interstates in my white 1995 Infiniti G-20, she Thelma, I Louise, on the Wal-Mart tour of America, crashing Motel 6 long after the lobby closes, hitting the continental buffet (cellophaned blueberry muffin: 23 grams fat), zipping through truck-stop cafes—she wondering why they don't sell *Hola* at the newsstand, and I wondering why they don't offer chair massages—dutifully tracing our journey with a well-creased road map on which the AAA lady marked 2,700 miles with a zesty orange Hi-Liter pen.

It's been, metaphorically, a trip. In my mother's eyes, it is the trip of a lifetime—well, the second trip of a lifetime, if you include last year's twenty-five-day, cross-country vacation. This time, her eyes glistened as we started across Mississippi, on the second day.

"I know this is the last time," she said in a drifting, little-girl voice, barely audible over the strains of Julio Iglesias's *Carretera*.

"Look, Mami," I interrupted, hoping to distract her, "Biloxi, sixteen miles."

She perked up right away at the thought, all those sparkling, gulf-docked casinos beckoning between massive, moss-draped oaks.

❧ ❧ ❧

We had been talking about everything and nothing at all, about the kinds of things that only could be discussed with strangers on an airplane, or on a long road trip, a safe zone, away from the Cuban rules of Miami.

She had repeated the stories and dreams of her hardscrabble childhood, how she, a carpenter's daughter, lulled herself to sleep each night imagining a future as a concert pianist or a declamatory poet on a velvet-curtained stage. But life in the sugar cane–fringed port town of Puerto Padre gave her only a fifth-grade education, long afternoon promenades around the town square, rations to be shared with four sisters and a brother. It also gave her the summer day on the beach when the son of a wealthy plantation owner decided aloud, upon watching her stroll the shore with her sisters, that he would marry her. That was my father. I was born a few years later, seventeen days after Fidel Castro's *barbudos* descended from the mountains.

Puerto Padre, with its narrow dirt roads and glorious, white-trunked royal palms, its florid cast of nicknamed characters—The Camel, The Goat, The Rabbit, along with the peanut vendor, the strumming troubadour who crooned outside Abuela Julia's open window, the poor slob who won the lottery and blew his fortune on shoes that didn't fit his gravel-beaten feet, the other poor slob who assembled a car in his living room, only to wonder how he'd drive it out—still glows in her memory forty years after she left it. She is never far from those chatty promenades and the sweet poverty of her youth, those days when a sumptuous dinner was marked by the lucky can of fruit she could score from her godmother, a Chinese woman who owned the town bakery.

～ ～ ～

"In my heart, you know, I'm still fifteen years old," she repeats her favorite phrase with a sigh. And I know it is true—she has always been that same little girl. No life experience has been powerful enough to erase this, not the abrupt exile from Cuba, the forced separation of nearly fifteen years from her parents, the arduous years in American sweatshops—first as a seamstress, then, deep into her fifties, as an assembly-line paper sorter in an inky print shop—the cruel, unpredictable swings of menopause, the cancer and all its ominous echoes.

When I was seven years old I was her interpreter, at school open houses, at doctors' offices, at the Kmart layaway counter. It took a divorce and some brutal soul searching to reconnect with my "inner *quinceañera*." Mami had no need for such a process—her birthday girl was always there, with bells on. At times I, the eldest of her three children, seemed more like the wary adult chaperoning her escapades, not the other way around. Always dazzled by celebrity, she'd drag me to the stage door after Julio Iglesias concerts so she could catch a glimpse of him. Her fascination with *la farándula* caused me to blush more than once. There was the time when she cornered Oscar de la Hoya and ordered him to stop boxing, to spare his *"cara linda."* There was the time I was interviewing her idol, Julio, at his island mansion and opened my bag only to find my mother had slipped a copy of his autobiography with this note: *"Lizi, favor pedirle a Julio un autógrafo . . ."* And there was the bouquet-filled afternoon following the Pulitzers, when Julio sent me a spectacular arrangement. "Hey!" shouted a co-worker at the sight of a young man carting that arrangement away. "Aren't those your Julio flowers?" Indeed, Mami had dispatched my brother, Eddie, to fetch the flowers so she "could water them for me."

~ ~ ~

Such memories charted our trip across America. We also dissected my late grandmother's obsession with race. I could never reconcile Abuela Julia's fear of blackness—how could she have claimed to love me, the granddaughter with the "bad," African hair, and fear everything negro? It turns out, my mother told me, Abuela's parents banished their son, Abuela's brother, when he married a black woman and fathered a slew of *mulaticos*. It turns out Abuela was the only one in her family who dared to travel to Havana to visit the outcast grandchildren. She would swell proudly each time her young *negrito* nephews shouted out, "¡*Tía, Tía!*"

For real? I softly gasped, allowing a warm ache to spread through my chest. Ay, *mi abuelita*.

After a polite pause, my mother returned the skewers: "As if you're one to talk about racism—you don't even look at a man if he's white."

She smiled all the way to Biloxi.

I watched her amid the bustle of the Grand Casino, ready to rock the house in her New Balance sneakers and her fanny pack. Her eyes darted around as I rattled off the rules: 1) Don't wander away from this section; 2) Don't forget to drink your water; 3) Don't forget to pee—the ladies' room is right by the Black Tie machines.

I followed her wispy gray head as she wove through the foreign bustle, oblivious to the garish trappings of the American casino culture. Doesn't she see it? I wondered as she set down her plastic bucket of quarters next to a glassy-eyed redhead who robotically hit the "spin" button on her Lucky Sevens machine, a cigarette dangling from her tangerine lips. My mother, lost in her delightful carnival, didn't appear to notice when the woman coughed up a knot of phlegm into the remains of her cocktail. In a casino, Mami's in another world, bless her soul. Where I see drunks and fat people, she sees neon rainbows. Where I hear the head-splitting clanging of empty promises, she hears the seductive jangle of possibility.

In the heat of the game, her eyes fire up, her breath quickens, her cheeks turn rosy. It's this way with any game, when she scratches lottery tickets, when she plays dominoes with her seven-year-old granddaughter, when she sits glued to the TV, clicking between her *telenovela* and the Miami Heat game. She got it from her father, this thrill for game. She scours dreams and daily life for lotto clues. To her, the three mice I found years ago in my kitchen did not constitute a pest problem—it was a Cash 3 opportunity.

"Play number 29," she urged, consulting La Charada China, the dream-inspired numbers game. "Mouse is 29."

I eventually did—and I lost. She said I waited too long. Her sister had followed her advice and won. *Tía* once dreamed someone whispered to her, "El 21. El 21." She played number 21 on Cash 3 at my mother's insistence, and, bingo!

Sure, there have been stunning losses. Just a few days ago, in fact, I found Mami slumped on a stool at the MGM Grand in Vegas. She had played away that night's allotment—two hours earlier. No more slots until morning, she vowed.

"*Vamos.*" She took my arm. "Let's go to the buffet."

B ut there is enough magic in her memories to keep her going for the gold—the time we won a car in the church raffle, the time a relative won $16,000 in a pyramid game and, of course, bought a Cadillac.

It is those magical glimmers that will carry us through Utah and into Colorado, where she will discover, at a tourist information pit stop in Vail, that—voilà!—there's a budding casino industry in Central City and Blackhawk, places I've never heard of.

"More casinos, Mami?" I will scold her. I mean, it's not like we hadn't hit every slot machine from Miami to Missouri. We played Biloxi, Gulf Port, New Orleans, Shreveport, an Indian casino in New Mexico, Vegas—hello!—Reno, and every jerkwater town in Nevada.

"But it's so close—look," she'll coax, signaling a squiggly hyphen of a road. "When will I ever see Colorado again?"

I will curse myself all the way up the winding road to Central City, lamenting my lack of spine and the inescapable symbiosis that caused me to travel such distances. If Mami got a cold, I'd sneeze. That's the way it always is with us.

When an infant grows, its mother stops lactating. Her milk-depleted breasts receive all the blows through the years—when her child suffers, when her child weeps, when her child leaves the nest. The cancer comes from loving so much it sears her insides. The life-sustaining milk, one way or another, is always there.

But is it supposed to work the other way around, too? I will seek no answers on the twisting mountain road to the next casino. As the highway gets steeper and the night gets darker, shrouding the mountains in drizzly, misty veils, I will pray in the thick silence between Mami and me. It will be well past 10 p.m. when we arrive in the old mining village where the narrow streets are crammed with vehicles and every saloon and casino seems to be busting at the seams.

"Central City, Mami," I will announce stiffly, pulling up at the only hotel in town. "I'll get a room."

But it will not be so easy—there will be no vacancy at the hotel. Mami will burst into tears and beg my forgiveness for this odyssey. She will be harder on herself than I could ever be, smacking the dashboard with the tourist brochure, offering to drive us back down the mountain. She will tremble like a little girl.

"That's okay, Mami, let's park and go inside anyway," I will say, trying to calm her, escorting her into the main casino and depositing her at her favorite machine. "*Mira*, the Wild Rose."

After twenty minutes on the phone, I will find a kindly bed-and-breakfast owner who offers to drive down and get me. I will leave Mami in the casino while I go with the woman in her black pick-up truck to take a look at her place, the Gingerbread Cottages. On the way up a steep drive, the woman will marvel at my journey.

"You are so wonderful to bring your mother here," she will enthuse. "You don't know how lucky you are."

The words of this stranger will gust in with angelic force on that frosty night. "You know I just lost my mother to lung cancer," she will go on, "I was so very close to her. What I would give to do what you are doing now. Enjoy every minute with her. She is a treasure."

Her words will be prophetic, for soon enough, when we return to Miami, doctors will find Mami's latent breast cancer spreading into her lungs, setting off exhausting cycles of chemotherapy and a debilitating struggle.

B ut we will have plenty of time to play Central City, settle into the Gingerbread Cottages, and savor all the quaintness of the mountains in the morning.

Miles away from home, Mami will continue to seek her jackpot fortunes. And I will thank my lucky stars for mine.

Ilan Stavans's mother, Ofelia

"To this day, I see each of my achievements as a confirmation of my mother's prophecies."

ৎৎৎৎৎৎৎৎৎৎ ILAN STAVANS

Ilan Stavans teaches at Amherst College. He is editor-in-chief of Hopscotch: A Cultural Review. *His books include* The Hispanic Condition *(HarperPerennial),* The Riddle of Cantinflas: Essays on Hispanic Popular Culture *(University of New Mexico Press),* The Oxford Book of Jewish Stories *and* On Borrowed Words: A Memoir of Language *(Viking). He has been awarded the Latino Literature Prize and a Guggenheim Fellowship and was nominated for the National Book Critics Circle Award. His work has been translated into half a dozen languages.*

September 19, 1985

I dial again, but without success. I'm consumed by anxiety. *Dios mío,* why doesn't anyone pick up? It is her voice I most want to hear. I don't know what to do with myself. Turn the TV on once more? I mustn't let myself become overwhelmed by the graphics of catastrophe. CNN broadcasts nothing but old reports. There will be no new satellite images until all communication has been resumed.

Impatient, apprehensive, I move from the kitchen to my bedroom. I look out the window. But I see nothing. I'm too distracted.

I spot a pile of photographs on the bookshelf. The top one is of my brother Darián in his early twenties, after a piano recital. Then comes one of my sister Liora next to my mother, both of them wearing *kovah tembles* in Tel Aviv. I flip the picture to see my father dressed up like a nineteenth-century London butcher in the Mexican adaptation of the musical *Sweeney Todd*. And next . . . next I see my mother, alone, proud, lovable, under a canopy of bougainvillea.

I study her enigmatic smile.

"To save a single soul," says the Talmud, "is to save the world entire." How many people lay dead in the streets of my native Ciudad de México? The earthquake struck four hours ago, at 7:25 a.m., local time. Why can't I get in touch with her? Where is everyone? Shouldn't I be with them, amid the chaos? What good am I, here in New York, so far away? Has she been swallowed by the earth's tremors? If so I beg you, almighty God, please be merciful in the suffering you inflict on your creature.

Photographs, what are they worth in these hours of darkness? But I ought to be more positive, so I look at them again. On average, how many does a family accumulate during a lifetime? Hundreds, sometimes even thousands. My mother has even more than most people. She is a bit like Ernest Hemingway. She believes that wherever she goes, there ought to be a camera to freeze the moment. How many times have I made fun of her? "And why do you need doubles?" I ask her. "To have them ready for when you get married," she replies. "I'm sure your wife will want to make albums." Will she, I wonder?

I stumble on a truism: most of my family photographs— surely most of the photos of my mother—were taken outside Mexico. It surprises me, because I had never thought of her as an itinerant person. On the contrary, by nature she is and always has been *un pilar de certidumbre*. Her parents were immigrants from Poland—her mother from Warsaw, her father from the shtetl Katchevate. But the exodus bug never bit her. She grew up loving Mexico, *y ahora está en su sangre*. And yet, I have pictures of her in Canada, Costa Rica, Spain, France, Scotland, Japan, Czechoslovakia. No sooner does the opportunity arise, and she is out and about: with my father, mostly, but also by herself or with friends. I, instead, left Mexico in my midtwenties and, aside from a few intervals, have lived abroad ever since. Like her forebears but unlike her, I'm an emigrant.

I leave the apartment for a walk. It is three o'clock in the afternoon. Did I have chores to do? Friends greet me sympathetically on the street. "I heard the awful news on the radio. Is everyone safe down at home?"

Down at home? The words cling to my ears. What does "down" mean? I ask myself. In hell? And "home." Has its meaning been abruptly redefined?

Someone else asks, "You've been hit twice in a matter of months, haven't you? Didn't a friend of yours die in a plane crash only a few months ago?"

I smile politely. No, I haven't heard anything yet, and, to be honest, I'm delighted with the silence, am I not? No news is good news.

But I feel uneasy. Isn't ours the age of technology? Shouldn't one be able to get in touch with friends and family by simply pressing a button? An ordained rabbi asks specifically about my mother. He met her not long ago.

I ask myself why she is more in my mind than my father or my siblings or . . .

I remember, as a little boy, staying up late to make sure my mother had reached home safely. Her unremitting love for me, I was convinced, gave me strength. If anything bad ever happened to me, I knew she would go to the end of the world to help. *Hasta el fin del mundo.* My fear of losing her was far deeper than my fear of losing my father, simply because of her steadfastness.

Steadfastness, solidity. I see my mother as a gravitational center.

From an office phone, I reach an international operator: *"Disculpe, señor,"* she says in an unpolluted Spanish. I ask her when the line might be restored. *"Nadie sabe."* No one knows.

The line, the umbilical cord. Don't firstborns spend a lifetime trying to cut it? To this day, I see each of my achievements as a confirmation of my mother's prophecies. Shortly before my departure for New York, she mapped my journey like a treasure hunter, assuring me that to dream is no sin.

"Make the most of yourself, for that is all there is of you," wrote Ralph Waldo Emerson, and my mother added in Yiddish: *Du darfts zeyn vos ich chob kein mol nisht geven.* You shall become what I never was. She was born in Mexico in the middle of the Second World War, in the year when the Nazi death camps became operational in Poland. Historian Lucy S. Dawidowicz estimates that at that time, about half a million Jews died as a result of hunger, disease, and hard labor, and many more began to be deported to Auschwitz and Treblinka. By 1942, Heinrich Himmler had declared that all ghettos must be destroyed. History is a wheel of fortune.

Mexico instead of Poland. She nurtured no nostalgia for the *shtetlech* of her father and those like him. As Maurice Samuel wrote in his book *Little Did I Know,* those Eastern European Jewish villages were "forlorn little settlements in a vast and hostile wilderness, isolated alike from Jewish and non-Jewish centers of civilization, their tenure precarious, their structure ramshackle, their spirit squalid." But the climate of the Mexican-Jewish community, in her eyes, was not much different: self-enclosed, suffocating—another shtetl of sorts. Why would anyone want to live there, either?

She was thirsty for knowledge and the ghetto displeased her. Almost without exception, upper-middle-class Mexican Jewish women of her generation never opened a book during high school, let alone after. She had been educated in a Yiddish school and kept kosher through her adolescence.

Then she met my father. With him she rebelled, but always within boundaries. They became engaged while she was quite young—not yet nineteen—and children came in quick succession. Unlike her girlfriends, she chose as her spouse neither a doctor nor a businessman but an actor, a man whose economic resources were nil. *Una bohemia,* she heard her girlfriends describe her, *bohemia y descarrilada.* Bohemian, and gone astray.

In the photographs I've seen of her in those days, she dressed like Greta Garbo: a silk scarf around her hair and neck, fashionable sunglasses, and a French novel in hand. She was not her husband's right arm, though. Their love, to flourish, needed to be based on equality, which meant sharing the responsibility of maintaining moral and economic order in their home. At night she filled small glasses with homemade yogurt, to be sold next morning to delicatessens as a way of supplementing the family income. Later she worked as a nurse at a clinic near our house.

The moment her second child came into the world, she went back to school and earned a bachelor's degree, then went on to graduate school. She became a psychotherapist, taught courses at the university, read Martin Buber's *I and Thou*, practiced yoga, studied the kabbalah and wrote a book about psychology and theater. But for some reason she stopped short of reaching higher in the academic hierarchy, even though she had the potential. Did she lack the tools? Did the mores of the times hold her back?

A s a young man, I strove for independence. My mother's torch of promise? Not until after I tested the limits of freedom. Leo Rosten, in *The Joys of Yiddish*, tells this tale: A Yid-dishe *mame* sent her son off to his first day in school with the usual pride and precautionary advice: "So, *bubeleh*, you'll be a good boy and obey the teacher? And you won't make noise, *bubeleh*, and you'll be very polite and play nice with the other children. And when it's time to come home, you'll button up warm, so you won't catch cold, *bubeleh*. And you'll be careful crossing the street and come right home, *bubeleh*." Off went the little boy. When he returned that afternoon, his mother hugged him and kissed him and asked, "So, did you like school, *bubeleh*? You made new friends? You *learned* something?" "Yeah," said the boy. "I learned that my name is Irving."

My mother never addressed me as *bubeleh*, but by a similar term of endearment: *tateleh*. It took a while for her to distinguish between *tateleh* and Irving and for me to face my own limitations.

In mid 1982, frustrated by routine, banging my head against a wall, I dropped out of college, sold my belongings, bought a small typewriter, and sailed the Atlantic to write, write, write. But I was struck by artistic paralysis and other than a couple of short stories and endless letters home, the journey produced little. My mother had placed all her hopes in me. "Better to test yourself now than build a life of doubt."

A life of doubt. Six months later, I came back *como el perro con la cola entre los patas*, "like a dog with his tail between his legs," contrite and empty-handed and resigned to a future less than bright. For my mother, my impetuous return was devastating. Her dreams, I sensed, had crashed miserably. I had become a poet manqué.

New York is different. This time I'm determined to make good on my promises, to thrive, to prove her right. Will I?

It is seven-thirty in the evening. I spy a public phone in the park. I try reaching an operator again. And again, no luck. My heart beats faster. What if the earth has swallowed them all? What if all I have left are memories? I sit on the grass, lean back slowly, and a few minutes later I'm face down, my eyes and nose and mouth pressed into the grass. Bizarrely, as the day reaches its conclusion, I'm able to invoke only a single scene. It's from Isaac Babel's "Story of My Dovecot," about a pogrom in Odessa in 1905, seen from the viewpoint of a nine-year-old boy. Throughout his life the boy has longed for a dovecot. He worked hard for it. He has been an outstanding student, earning a place at a secondary school at a time when only a minuscule number of Jews are accepted. But in the crucial, haunting scene, just as he finally gets his pigeon at the market, everything collapses in the mayhem of the pogrom. He is dealt a flying blow, then lies motionless. "I lay on the ground, and the guts of the crushed bird trickled down from my temple. They flowed down my cheek, winding this way and that, splashing, blinding me. The tender pigeon guts slid down over my forehead, and I closed my solitary unstopped-up eye so as not to see the world that spread out before me. This world was tiny, and it was awful. A stone lay just before my eyes, a little stone so chipped as to resemble the face of an old woman with a large jaw. A piece of string lay far away, and a bunch of feathers that still breathed. My world was tiny, and it was awful. I closed my eyes so as not to see it, and pressed myself tight into the ground that lay beneath me in soothing dumbness."

I too pressed myself tight into the ground. My world was tiny. And I remember that my mother had confessed a secret. As a newlywed she had gone to an astrologer, eager to find out her fate. At one point the astrologer, while reading her chart, stopped cold. My mother looked into her face and saw only puzzlement. "I see a major calamity taking place in your family, although I cannot say when or whom it affects." Since then my mother has lived in fear, waiting for the prediction to come true.

The park is crowded with happy passersby. "To save a single soul," says the Talmud. I must rush back. CNN will surely have fresh satellite images by now. Half an hour later, I reach my apartment again. As I cross the threshold, I hear the phone ringing. I pick it up. First comes a strange voice, then a familiar one. *"Tateleh?"*

"¡Mamá, bendita seas! ¿Cómo están todos?" I scream into the receiver, pushing the future back on track.

Jaime Manrique's mother, Soledad Reina, in Tampa, Florida,
1977, after she was sworn in as an American citizen
at the age of seventy-eight

"The legend of her beauty spread along the towns of the Magdalena river."

Jaime Manrique was born and raised in Colombia. He is the author of the novels Colombian Gold *(Clarkson Potter)*, Latin Moon in Manhattan *(St. Martin's Press), and* Twilight at the Equator *(Faber and Faber). His most recent works are his poetry collection* My Night with Federico García Lorca *(Painted Leaf Press)*, Sor Juana's Love Poems *(translated with Joan Larkin), and his autobiography,* Eminent Maricones: Arenas, Lorca, Puig, and Me *(University of Wisconsin Press). He has been a teacher at Columbia University, the New School for Social Research, and Mount Holyoke College.*

A Mother Named
Queen Solitude

My mother's name is Soledad. After she married her last husband, Mr. Reina, a semiretired Italian-American mobster, her name became Soledad Reina, Queen Solitude.

My mother was born to Serafina Ardila and José Ardila (they were cousins) in the hamlet of Barranco de Loba, the she-wolf's ravine, a *palenque* by the shores of the Magdalena River in

Colombia. *Palenques* were settlements made by runaway slaves who escaped to remote areas during colonial times. My grandmother is illiterate, a black woman, but my grandfather could read and write and was of mixed blood, a mestizo. Serafina and José had two children out of wedlock. Eventually, my grandfather married a light-skinned educated woman. To his credit, instead of abandoning his "love children" (which is the custom in Colombia), he took my mother to live with his new family. Because my mother is guarded about her past, I don't know the exact circumstances under which she left her mother's house. Of those years she has told me only one thing: When she was a girl my grandfather would send her out with a large tray on her head to go from house to house selling little sugared candies (the kind of candies that the Buendía women made in *One Hundred Years of Solitude* to support the family). One day, mother tripped and overturned the tray, strewing the candies on the sand. As punishment, my grandfather hanged her by the wrists from the beams on the living room ceiling.

Soledad was a ravishing beauty. In the pictures I've seen of her in her early thirties, when she was living with my father, it's as though one of Gauguin's Tahitian women had gone to Paris to model for Balenciaga or Coco Chanel.

Before Mother met my father, it seems she married a man by the name of Leal. This I infer from surviving telegrams my father sent to Soledad Ardila de Leal. In an album of old photos that my mother kept until about ten years ago, there was a picture of an elaborately dressed young child in a coffin. This child may have been a product of her first marriage.

The year I turned forty, I went to visit my grandmother, who is over a hundred years old and still lives in Barranco de Loba. I decided it was the right time to ask her about how my parents had met. She told me that Mother met my father when she went to Barranquilla "to sew." She offered no more information. In any case, my father, Gustavo Manrique, was twenty years my mother's senior, and married to a member of one of Santa Marta's most prominent families. I know my parents met in October of 1944 because, to this day, my mother has kept a series of letters and telegrams my father sent to her over a period of ten years.

My father was a banana baron. His plantations were located in the stretch of land between Santa Marta and the town of Ciénaga. This is the region Gabriel García Márquez immortalized in his early books, and the setting of his magnificent masterpiece, *One Hundred Years of Solitude*.

Mother's greatest asset was her beauty. I've heard from her relatives that the legend of her beauty spread along the towns of the Magdalena River and many men came by my grandfather's house from nearby towns to ask for her hand in marriage.

My father was wealthy and had an ancient aristocratic name. I don't think my mother understood how ancient and aristocratic the Manrique name is—she has only a second-grade education. Colombians have asked me: "Are you one of the good or the bad Manriques?" The "bad ones," I assume, are the Manriques who do not belong to Colombia's aristocracy. The "good ones" are an offshoot of the Manriques whose name goes back to the days of the Holy Roman Empire, and who, under the leadership of Don Rodrigo Manrique, freed Castile from the Moors shortly before Christopher Colombus sailed for the New World. Don Rodrigo was the father of Captain Jorge Manrique, one of the most famous and influential Spanish poets of all time, whose philosophical epic poem, *Couplets on the Death of My Father* (c. 1475), is one of the peaks of world poetry. These are also the Manriques whose portraits, painted by Goya, hang in the Metropolitan Museum of Art in New York, and who, at least in nineteenth-century Colombia, produced notable men of letters, government, and the army. "The pen and the sword" seems to have been the family motto. All my mother knew was that my father was rich and white, and that his family was one of the best families of Bogotá, and that he adored her.

His adoration is clear in the letters he sent her during the eleven years they were together. In these letters, in which he often addresses her as "*mi negrita adorada,*" "my darling little black one," he proves himself a true Manrique. Rereading them as a grown man, I understand that I am a writer because of my father. The letters are searingly passionate and sensual: he praises my mother's beauty and elegance, and obsessively names her the object of his deepest affection.

Although they were a couple for eleven years, they never lived together. He set her up at one of his banana plantations on the outskirts of the town of Río Frío, "cold river." The river after which the town is named flows down from the snow-capped summit of the Sierra Nevada of Santa Marta and its swift waters are deep, sparkling like diamonds, and icy. For a few years, my parents made that plantation their love nest. I wasn't born in Río Frío, but I have vague memories of my visits to the farm when I was a toddler. My mother lived in a two-story clapboard house, an imitation of the southern plantation homes the United Fruit Company built in that area. I remember seeing pictures taken of her at around this time. She is riding a white horse, wearing boots, khaki pants, an embroidered shirt, and a cowboy hat, and holding a hunting rifle. Because my father's wife and children were in Santa Marta where he kept his exporting office, he only came to visit my mother on weekends or when he had pressing business to take care of at the plantation.

She must have been lonely when my father wasn't with her, because she surrounded herself with a retinue of women: her cook, Isidora, a black woman she loved as if she were her own mother; Anastasia, my mother's goddaughter; Aunt Emilia, who became my godmother; and Aunt Aura, who was one of my grandfather's illegitimate children, as my mother herself was. When Mother heard that Aunt Aura was living with her mother, who worked as a maid in Barranquilla, Mother offered to bring up the young girl and send her to school. Some years ago I asked why she had done that. "She was my sister, after all," was her reply. "I couldn't let her live like that." Both Emilia and Aura went to school in Santa Marta and visited my mother during their vacations. Two of my mother's brothers (José Antonio, her full-blood brother, and José, who was my grandfather's eldest son by his wife), also came to study in Santa Marta and they also spent weekends at the plantation.

My father owned fighting cocks that were famous throughout the Caribbean. He traveled with them through the northern coast of Colombia to fight the cocks of the best *galleros*. The excellence of my father's birds was known as far away as Havana, where he took his best fighters to compete. Twenty years ago one of my aunts told me this story: My father had not come to visit my mother for a long time. Suspecting that he had taken a new mistress in another city, Mother sent him an ultimatum. "Come back right away, or you'll regret it." When he didn't show up on the appointed day, she gave orders to the overseer of the farm that, for every day my father was away, he should kill so many of the priceless roosters. When my father finally showed up, she had decimated his stable.

All her life my mother wanted desperately to have her father's approval. Cruel as he was, he had brought her into his own home, where she was given the respect due to the eldest daughter of a rich peasant, and in his house she learned the manners of a young lady. The love was reciprocated. My grandfather made sure that his legitimate children and his wife accepted and respected her. Maybe it was because she was his firstborn, or because she was the most beautiful of all his daughters, or the one who, although she was a scandal, ended up being the most adventurous and lived the most daring life.

Mother must have tired of the isolation of the plantation in Río Frío. Shortly before I was born, when my parents had already been a couple for five years, Mother moved to the town of Ciénaga, and after my birth she relocated to Barranquilla, the largest city on the Atlantic coast of Colombia.

Right after my birth, my parents' relationship soured. I suspect that for Gustavo Manrique, Soledad had represented a thrilling and forbidden romance without the tensions and responsibilities of children. But to my mother, my birth represented more than her great desire to have a child. Now she was not merely another mistress of the banana baron, but the mother of a Manrique. She was determined that I would be brought up like a prince—which also meant that she saw herself as the queen.

For the occasion of my baptism, an advertisement appeared in the social pages of two conservative newspapers, one in Bogotá, the other in Barranquilla. The advertisement said that Jaime Manrique Ardila, the son of Gustavo Manrique Álvarez and his wife Soledad Ardila de Manrique, had been baptized in Barranquilla. (Later, my mother would vehemently deny having had anything to do with the placement of those ads.) Both my parents thought the ads had been placed by enemies who wanted to hurt my father, because they publicly made him a bigamist. From the series of letters my father fired to my mother, it seems that many people all over Colombia saw the ads. The effect, he wrote her, was worse than that of "the atomic bomb." His wife and children had been humiliated. His business acquaintances stopped speaking to him, crossing the street when they ran into him. The banks of Santa Marta, where he conducted most his business, asked him to clarify the situation, threatening to close his accounts. After this incident, although they remained together for eight more years, their relationship chilled.

It should be harder for me to write the part of my mother's story in which I play no part. After all, that's her story and writing about it is an invasion of her privacy. But I find it nearly impossible to write about Mother after I entered her life, although I have every right to do it, since that part is also my narrative, and I own it. I have written about my relationship with my mother in my autobiography, *Eminent Maricones*. It's a book I could never show her. I know that the things I say in it would wound my mother. It saddens me to think that I'll never be able to show her the book in which this story appears, either. Over the years, she's repeatedly implored me to stop writing about her and my father. Yet, it is only because I've continued writing about them—about us—that I've finally been able to free myself from the past and to become a man.

I've always spoken of my mother as a romantic figure, a woman larger than life—which she is, at least to her children and grandchildren. With the passage of time, however, I've come to see her not just as the woman who could hold men in thrall with her beauty, the woman who overcame her humble origins to travel a great distance from the place where she was born, but as the other woman she also is, a woman who has suffered, struggled, and survived.

I give credit to my mother for many things. After my parents separated my father made no effort to see me or my sister. If mother hadn't sent us to visit him in his office a couple of times a year, I would have no memories of him, unpleasant though many of them are. Mother also made sure that my sister and I received an education.

Having been brought up in Colombia's *machista* culture, it must have been difficult for her to be the mother of a homosexual son. Her brothers as well as many other members of her family are homophobic. I am sure that she has had occasion to defend her gay son.

When I was a boy she was horrified that I was a sissy, that I formed deep attachments to other boys, that I was expelled from school at age five for asking another boy to show me his penis. It must have been awkward for her to explain to her family and to many of her friends that, for sixteen years, I lived with another man. And it must have been disappointing that her only son never made her a grandmother. Yet the same mother who, until I was in my twenties, disapproved of my sexuality, today is proud of me and accepts gay people. She has changed so much that when I separated from my lover she was deeply worried that I had broken up my home and was alone in the world.

It's been twenty-five years since I moved away from Tampa, Florida, where my mother, a widow, now lives in a community of senior citizens. Nowadays, though we speak often on the phone, I am someone who visits her once a year. I am her son, and a stranger. But this estrangement has allowed me to see her objectively so that I can now appreciate her many qualities. Only a woman with great inner resources could have lived the life she led in Colombia, a country where most unmarried women with children were seen as pariahs. Still, she won the respect and admiration of upstanding people in Colombia.

When I visit her now, I am astounded by her wide and varied circle of friends. Her telephone rings all the time. She has friendships with men and women, old and young, and she rushes to the side of any one of them when they are sick or dying or in need of company or advice. Many old people become reclusive, depressed, and lose interest in life. Not my mother. When she was seventy-five she went alone to visit relatives in a jungle town in Venezuela. Ever since I can remember, my mother has been my grandmother's sole means of support. For the past fifty years, she's made sure that her mother has never gone hungry. The house in which my grandmother lives was a present my mother gave her while she was still living with my father. When my mother was seventy-eight she became an American citizen because she wanted to show her gratitude to the country that has given so much to her and to her children. For the past couple of years she has lived in a tenth-floor apartment overlooking the Hillsborough River. On her balcony, Mother has created a sanctuary where pigeons come to roost. When her friends visit, they sit in the living room discussing recipes for the best preparation of the baby pigeons.

No passion has lasted longer in my life than my passion for writing. I must have been ten years old when I read *Couplets on the Death of My Father* in a schoolbook, and I suspected that with a name like mine, and because there were writers in my father's family, I could not grow up to be anything else. One day when I was eleven or twelve I ran through the front door to find my mother on her wicker rocking chair reading the newspaper. I informed her that my Spanish teacher had said I would be a writer when I grew up. (He said this because I could make up fantastic lies.) Up until that moment, since I was a bright and grandiose brat, it had been assumed I would grow up to be President of Colombia. There was, after all, the precedent of Marco Fidel Suárez, an illegitimate child who was one of Colombia's most illustrious presidents. Instead of discouraging my desire to be a writer, Mother was happy that I was going to be a "journalist." Writer, journalist, it was the same to both of us.

Looking back, my admiration for my mother was greatest at about the time we immigrated to the United States. At the age of forty-seven, never having held a job, she moved to a country where she had only one friend, a country whose language she did not speak. In the years before she met her American husband, my mother worked in a factory as a seamstress, she took care of old people, and she cleaned houses. Often she held two or three jobs at a time, never complaining, so that she could make a home for my sister and me. It was the first time in her life that she had not depended on a man to support her and her children. As soon as we settled down in Tampa, she began to arrange passage for her relatives who also wanted to move to the United States. When I received a scholarship to go to college, Mother (unlike the parents of so many immigrants I knew) never insisted that I become a lawyer, a doctor or an accountant. She respected my desire to become a writer.

In my twenties, when I left home and went off to find my own place in the world, Mother sent me a weekly allowance to be sure I could survive on part-time jobs and begin to write my books. By that time, she was married to Mr. Reina, a lovely man of whom I grew fond.

Unfortunately, I turned out to be a Freudian writer and a satirist. The protagonist of my first novel was a semiautobiographical character who murders his father—a father very much like my own. My mother was horrified with the book. Her only comment after she read it was: "*¡Qué horror! ¡Qué horror!*" Just about everything I've written since then has horrified her. After I began to write fiction in English, she must have been relieved that she could no longer read my work. Even so, she often advises me about my career. "Why don't you write about nice things, like García Márquez?" But one of the qualities that recurs in my writing, my dark sense of humor, is something I seem to have inherited from my mother. Recently I sent her a copy of *Cromos*, Colombia's version of *People* magazine, in which my picture appeared across two pages. Since Colombia is still the country that Mother cares about most, I thought she'd be proud to see her son getting such a big spread. When a week went by and I hadn't heard from her, I called to find out if she'd received the magazine. She had. "You look fat," she said. "You'd better lay off those pies."

Much of my writing is autobiographical. In my novels, my poems, and my memoirs, the figure of my mother is a haunting presence. When my last book of poems appeared in Spanish, a volume in which I had selected my poetry of the last twenty years, I was surprised to find how many poems were about her. My father is the one with the famous literary name, but it is my mother who is the source of much of my poetry. My poems about her are, I think, "lovely," "nice." Any mother should be happy with them. I sent her the book as a tribute, to show her my love. This time, I thought, she would approve.

"Please stop writing nasty things about me," she said, by way of reviewing my collection. "Don't you have anything better to write about? Do you think García Márquez would have become famous writing about his mother? No wonder your books don't sell!"

The most wonderful tribute I can pay to my mother is to say that whereas most children automatically love their mothers, I've grown to love Soledad.

Francisco Goldman's mother, the former Mercedes Yolanda Molina Hernández, photographed in the early 1950s

"I want everyone to look at the photograph of my mamita and marvel that I could have sprung from the womb of such a beauty!"

Francisco Goldman is the author of two novels: The Long Night of White Chickens *(Atlantic Monthly Press) won the Sue Kaufman Award for First Fiction from the American Academy of Art and Letters;* The Ordinary Seaman *(Atlantic Monthly Press) was a finalist for the PEN/Faulkner award and the International IMPAC Dublin Fiction Prize, and was named one of the "Best 100 American Books of the Century" by the* Hungry Mind Review. *As a contributing editor for* Harper's *magazine, he covered Central America in the 1980s. His work has appeared in many magazines, including* The New Yorker *and the* New York Times Magazine. *A recipient of a 1998 Guggenheim Foundation grant, Goldman is currently at work on his third novel.*

¡Mamita Linda!

Somebody once asked Gabriel García Márquez to write an introduction to a book about Che Guevara, and he answered along the lines of, all right, except he'd need about a thousand pages and ten years to do it. I have to admit that I feel similarly when it comes to writing about my mami. Like any other person with a sense of privacy, self-respect, and propriety—and my mother is nothing if not possessed of those things—she is not going to like being publicly written about, no matter what I end up saying.

One reason I am doing this, Mamita, is I want everyone to see your picture. I want everyone to look at the photograph of my mamita and marvel that I could have sprung from the womb of such a beauty! I've been promised that this essay will be accompanied by a photograph. The Mexican writer Salvador Elizondo—so goes a story I heard—once received a similar promise from a newspaper that was going to publish an essay he'd written about his parakeet. But when the essay ran, it was without the photograph. Incensed, Elizondo phoned the editor to protest. The editor was duly apologetic, but couldn't help asking Elizondo why it was so important to him, anyway. And Elizondo answered that the only reason he'd written the essay in the first place was so that later he'd be able to hold the newspaper up to his parakeet and say, *Look, perico, your picture's in the paper!*

Once, my mother boasted, "The only thing I ever did wrong as a mother was not getting braces for you." Totally true, Mami! Crooked lower teeth aside, you cannot be blamed for any other of my innumerable shortcomings. On the other hand, I know that if you were ever to compile such a list, near the very top would be the shameless way in which I occasionally exploit and expose family secrets.

My mother's full maiden-name is Mercedes Yolanda Molina Hernández. She is casually known as Yolanda, or Yoli. She was born sometime before the Second World War, in Guatemala City, when it was still, in the antiquated phrase, a "little cup of silver." Then, it was a beautiful and provincial plateau capital nestled between volcanoes and mountains, not the ever-spreading, poverty, violence, corruption and pollution-blighted

Central American megalopolis it has since become. In the courtyard of the Spanish-colonial house in the old city center where she grew up, my mother kept the pet monkey and fawn I never tired of hearing stories about when I myself was a child, including the sad one about how the monkey died, having wedged a coffee cup over its own little head. Abuelita had opened a hat store called York, the first of my grandparents' stores, which sold ladies' hats copied from American and European fashion magazines. At home, a room off the courtyard held a busy little workshop where young women and one fondly recalled, though "doubtful," young man were employed making artificial flowers for the hats. Abuelita had been the daughter of a poor immigrant from Spain who, in his late middle-age, had become a wealthy cattle rancher on the south coast. Her mother, my great-grandmother, was a much younger girl, the "flower" of that village, a full-blooded Mayan—or certainly *not* full-blooded, depending on who in my family is telling the story. She died, very young, in childbirth, and *el patrón* Hernández died soon after that. The male descendants inherited his ranches, and Abuelita and her sister, Tía Nano, went to live in a boarding house/finishing school in the capital, run by French spinster sisters. Francisco Molina, "Abuelito," was the illegitimate but recognized offspring of a Guatemalan colonel and a certain *dama* whom no one has ever actually told me anything about. Who were these two great-grandmothers of mine, my own mamita's abuelas? Why the mystery and silence? *¿Quién sabe?* Because of the usual cast-iron Guatemalan proprieties, of course. And probably something to do with an absence of European pedigree. Most Molinas have very Mayan noses and eyes, short necks or even no necks, and squarish torsos. Yet my mother and I share coarse, curly hair, which is certainly not Indian. Hers is reddish.

The majority of Guatemalans, of course, are pure Mayan, and very few people who are born in that country do not have at least some of those ancient American genes. Anyone in Guatemala who is not an Indian living according to traditional Indian ways is called a *ladino*. Wealth has traditionally been rooted in a more or less feudal plantation economy. And the *ladino* Guatemalans, most of whom live in the capital—whether middle-class merchants or the fabulously wealthy rulers of coffee *fincas*—have often been described as possessing the character of a settlers' colony within a conquered and ruthlessly administered country.

Many of the most prominent coffee planters in Guatemala were German. In the years leading up to the Second World War, pro-Nazi and German pride were openly displayed in the capital: balls, pro-Nazi election rallies, and marches. Guatemala's dictator, General Jorge Ubico, sympathized with his European fascist counterparts, but he knew how the future's hemispheric power alignment was shaping up, and declared war on Germany immediately after the United States did. He expelled the Germans and seized their coffee plantations. In 1944, General Ubico was toppled, ushering in Guatemala's golden decade of reformist and even revolutionary democracy, which was ended, the very year I was born, by the United Fruit Company and the CIA in the coup of 1954.

I mention all this because this was the atmosphere in which my mother came of age. It's not hard to imagine the sort of prejudices to which anyone raised inside such a "colony" would be exposed. The Molina-Hernández family did not own plantations. Our family business, long after the hat store closed, was selling baby clothes and imported toys. But those stores were successful. My abuela, Doña Hercilia, was a strong matriarchal character, known to everybody in town. When I look at photographs of my mother's youth, I am struck by the air of tropical elegance and sophistication, by the stylish beauty of the men and women and their air of unaffected gaiety. The photographs capture the atmosphere of a colony in the purest sense of the word, insulated and protected from the ugliness of the world. There are photos of costume parties and plantation outings on horseback, beauty pageants, waterskiing on the lake. There are women posing in bathing suits, hands raised to hold their big hats, elbows in the air, one leg forward, lipsticky smiles, somehow managing to look as glamorous as Rita Hayworth but virginal at the same time. The men wear debonair pencil mustaches like Mexican crooner–movie stars. Or they affect Humphrey Bogart's hard-boiled yanqui swagger.

This is the young woman my abuelos sent to study in the new promised land, the United States. My tío Hugo was at the University of California in Berkeley, where he studied business and immersed himself in the can-do work and political ethic of the "Good Neighbor" U.S.A. before coming home to assume the family business. My mother was sent to San José State, to be near him. My abuelos wanted her out of Guatemala. In time-honored Latin American tradition, she had been sent abroad to remove her from a tragically inappropriate love. (Now I am spilling secrets again and I am really going to get it.) I don't like looking at my mother's photo album. Too many boyfriends! She says they're not boyfriends, they're friends, friends of her brothers', because brothers and sisters and their friends all chastely hung around together like that back then. I sit at home on the couch when I visit and look through the album and shout out, "Look at this one, *ay no*, Mami, what a *mamón*, how could you?!!" Who's the guy in a flight suit standing under the wing of a U.S. Air Force bomber at an Alaskan airbase? What is she doing in that apartment or dorm room or whatever, letting her picture be taken with that backdrop of cheesy pinup girls from magazines taped to the wall? She says those were just some guy's roommate's pinup pictures. And who cares? She didn't really care about either of them.

One night—this was in early 1977—I was home from college, and the cabinet of new U.S. Pres Jimmy Carter was being introduced on TV. Suddenly, my mother chirped in astonishment, "Zbiggy!" The future Secretary of State had carried her in his arms one night across a mud-puddled Harvard Yard after a foreign-student party, which is where she'd met him. My mother was living in Boston by then, in a boardinghouse for foreign women. (I guess Guatemala had been ruled still unsafe for her return.) She said, "Zbiggy was like a *lion!*" She said it like this: like a *lyyy-yun*. Zbiggy, huh?

Somehow Mamita ended up working as a secretary in a factory that primarily made false teeth. The Myerson Tooth Corporation, it was then called, before it was bought out by Pfizer. "*Chapinas*," you know, are late for everything—they are supposed to be. It's somehow part of being a well-brought-up damita to be late for everything—a nineteenth-century romantic version of ethereal femininity—and so my mother, after many kind warnings, was fired for being late to work every day. My father found her weeping by the water fountain just after she'd received the bad news.

Bert Goldman, from a Ukrainian Jewish immigrant family (where the surname was Malumudavich), was the chemical engineer who ran the lab that made the teeth. His pockets, like carnivore's caves, always held loose (false) teeth. Between the darkest useful false tooth and the whitest one range an infinite degree of hues, and that is the false-tooth engineer's domain and bane; to pursue, in the mundane colorations of everyday teeth, a rainbow of infinite shadings. A perfect match for every imperfect tooth! Often he'd journey to northern Canada, to quarries and mines, in search of perfect veins of feldspar (this before the teeth biz became plasticized). He was big, smart, gentlemanly, extremely athletic, and much older than she was.

Their wedding was going to be in Guatemala City, but at the last minute the ecclesiastical authorities (who, by the way, were then busily conspiring with the CIA in preparing the population for the coming coup) ruled that she couldn't marry a Jew in any of their churches. So the wedding party moved north to Mexico, though of course not everyone could make it. But at the church in Mexico City, bridesmaids—professional bridesmaids! credibly wholesome, pretty, and friendly young women—could be rented, for both the ceremony and the party afterwards. My mother remembers those bridesmaids very fondly.

Marital difficulties. Flight! I vaguely remember sleeping on chairs pushed together in Florida hotel rooms and taking Pan Am flights to the old Aurora Airport in Guatemala City, its terminal like a giant wood-carved pagoda. My infant sister and I lived in my abuelos' house, played in that same courtyard where the mischievous monkey had romped and died. I have many vivid memories of that time. How I was loved! By Mami, my abuelos, Tía Nano, godmothers, and an endless parade of maids, *niñeras*, and shopgirls! We were destined to go on living there, had not my sister and I contracted tuberculosis, precipitating a return to Boston and a marital rapprochement.

The suburbs. A little ranch house in a subdivision in a pretty New England valley. The neighbors were mostly Irish and Italian, solidly middle-class laborers and white-collar salesmen and such. After a documentary on Guatemala appeared on television, the neighbors went around saying that my mamita had grown up bathing naked and doing her laundry in rivers. Someone, who turned out to be the neighborhood pedagogue, told their children that because my father was Jewish, we worshipped a Golden Calf. Mamita would drive to the next town to attend Mass. And so on.

Boy, was I a wimp! I was not only sickly, but ridiculously, lovingly pampered and spoiled in the manner of any little boy from any of our countries who is exposed to a house full of doting women. That courtyard in my abuelos' house in Guatemala City was like a packed arena of feminine adoration with me at the center. ¡Ay, *mi amorcito, mi chulo, mi rey! ¿Qué quiere el niño más divino del mundo?* (How does such a culture produce such violent men? The answer is not as simple as it seems.) I had a very strong accent, and in second grade I was regularly pulled out of class for private sessions with a speech therapist ("Say mother." ". . . *mud-hair.*") And I was picked on. And was afraid. Especially afraid of *the ball,* any ball. Daddy, like I said, was a great athlete, and probably fed up. Anyway, he was working very hard, coming home tired. Whenever we played catch I crumpled as if he were Thor hurling hammers and thunderbolts. So I think of Mami—still so glamorous, in her shorts and dark glasses, a colorful scarf over her head and knotted loosely under her chin—at least that's how I remember her—out in the yard, trying to teach me to catch a baseball. Pathetic! As if she had any idea! The ball skidding past each of us, back and forth. Mami turning to chase the ball. Franky turning to chase the ball. *¡Jajaja!* . . .

So that I could learn to defend myself, she enrolled me in karate classes in Boston. The violent and bigoted neighborhood guerrilla war raging between parochial and public school kids was getting dangerous, indeed. They ambushed me on my way home from school one day, at the edge of the cemetery atop the hill overlooking our street. They had long bamboo poles with knives attached—what imaginations! Never before had I run so fast—or since! Those poles slowed them down. As if karate classes were going to help me with kids like that! I remember dressing in my new white pajamas, and bowing to the similarly outfitted little girl who'd been assigned to be my partner. She promptly flipped me—splat—on to the mat! Eventually I did catch on, not to karate but to boyhood, and, in all honesty, learned to love certain violent and fast sports, and became as outwardly thuggish as I needed to be.

This was not the life for which Mamita had been raised, inside the "little cup of silver." But this was how she embarked on her subsequent decades of American life. I still recall our summer visits to Guatemala as "flights" or "escapes" to a happier, more beautiful, and, for her, more natural place. And I thought of my Guatemalan family as "rich" compared to my U.S.A. one. My mother was always studying and working, and I probably assumed it was because of our need for money. In ways I was then totally oblivious of, she'd responded to her circumstances by developing and pursuing a new idea of herself. She didn't want to be a bilingual secretary; she wanted to teach. And eventually a Spanish teacher was what she became, first in adult education, then at a junior college in suburban Boston, and finally at the Berklee School of Music in Boston.

Still, there was a perhaps not unusual degree of unhappiness in our house. My father, with his strict Russian-Jewish peasant immigrant morality, was not well-suited to guiding adolescents through those dark, druggy, late–Vietnam War years. He had been the most overjoyed and loving dad during my childhood. But for much of my youth he was an enraged, frustrated, tragic, and violent man. My mother hovered somewhere in the background during those years, futile and helpless, forever calling, Don't hit him in the head! Without a doubt, I was a maddening kid, and provoked the hell out of him. I was unhappy at home and at school, and my mother always says that from the time I was thirteen on she hardly saw me anymore, that I basically lived in the street. I hardly remember my mother from those years. I was consumed by my battle with my father. And, with her ridiculous Guatemalan proprieties and prejudices, I thought my mother didn't have a clue! ("Remember," she never stopped telling us, "you're Guatemalan too!" Well, that was a big help. *That* was going to keep me out of fights.) My parents separated again when I was in high school. Years later, they reunited, and my father, long retired, is again as sweet as he was when I was a little boy.

¡Ay, *Mami!* What an idea I had of you! Temperamentally, we were always the most alike, you and I. Everyone thinks we're happy and easy and getting along fine, especially when we aren't. Who knew what was going on with you, throughout all those years, as you lived your hard-working American life, always the sweetly demure Guatemalan *dama*, never complaining or negative or resentful, while inside you'd become so complex and wise and watchful, all the time, keeping up that air not out of irremediable nostalgia and unrepentant provincialism but out of pride. It was a statement and a mask and a weapon. I had hardly any idea of it until recently, until that day in Washington, D.C. (My sister, Barbara, is the one who really knows you, who is closest to you, who has been there with you every step of the way.)

It was striking that my mother refused to become a U.S. citizen. This seemed to me to be a part of her indefatigable pride in her "silver cup" origins. And I suspected that there might be some kind of tax motive in it. It never really crossed my mind that there might be an element of defiant and disappointed protest in her refusal, because that wasn't like Mamita at all. Her Guatemalan identity was what mattered most to her, I thought. She remained a Guatemalan citizen, I thought, out of a somewhat self-deceiving, self-protective sense of pride rooted in a kind of fairy tale about her lost life, the life she would have had had she married there, stayed there, raised a family there, a world where traditionally men considered it an insult to their masculinity to allow their wives to work. (The world I suspected she secretly regretted losing!) Her close friends in the United States were Latin American, almost every one of them. Yet it was in her work, especially at the Berklee School of Music, that she was happiest, most fulfilled. I like to joke that she was the marimba teacher there, but no, she taught Spanish. At that wonderful school, famous for its jazz programs, my mother found her first true community in this country. The students came from all over the world. Much of the faculty, including the professor who hired her, is African-American. For twenty-five years, she was immersed in hipness, surrounded by sweet, ambitious, musical kids from all over, and by every cutting-edge generational ambience, every outrageous style and mode of behavior that should provoke in any well-brought-up *chapina* only a repulsed and censorious squawk of *¡Qué horror!* and shudders over horrible gringo libertinism and decadence.

A few years ago, Mamita suddenly became a U.S. citizen. Typically, she didn't offer any elaborate explanation. She giggled, and playfully waved around the little American flag they'd given her at the oath-taking ceremony. I was a bit disappointed. I had begun to like her stubborn and eccentric resistance. I didn't really know why she'd changed her mind, nor did I have any real opinion about it. In fact I didn't really have any idea, until last year, in Washington, D.C. I've published two novels, and both of them have been finalists for a prize given out at the Folger Shakespeare Library during a ceremony that is very beautifully done and would make any parent glow with pride. The first time, both my parents attended, and the second, because my father was ill, only my mother. During the party after the ceremony, she was speaking with two of the women who administer the prize. This is what I heard my *mamita* tell them: she had only decided to become a U.S. citizen after that first awards ceremony at the Folger Library because seeing her son so honored there and treated with such respect had made her finally feel accepted in the United States.

The prize administrators were startled and moved. I was totally blown away. I stood there gaping at her. Finally accepted! All those years, then, so quietly borne, feeling *not accepted!* What silent hurts, what searing perceptions, what down-and-dirty knowledge about *nuestro país* it all implies. I'd never even suspected that her experience was about such carefully weighed and conscious depths and that there was this nemesis, a United States in which she adamantly felt *not accepted.* So, step by step, year by year, methodically and studiously, she had become educated, had gained a profession, had weathered a marriage and family and sent children to college, had become the sort of modern American woman who even understood and admired the ways of wild and unconventional young musicians, who was comfortable around people from all backgrounds. My mother had finally become an American, on her own terms. That was what she had wanted. It had all mattered to her, greatly. (And she didn't really regret having lost her genteel life inside a "silver cup" after all! She knew she would have stifled there. *Mamita rebelde!*)

Mamita *linda*, in some ways yours is the only story that interests me. The mystery of human loneliness and dignity and love. The complicated mystery of our lives in our Americas.

Elizabeth Yolanda, mother of Dagoberto Gilb

*"I was small, probably just walking, and looking up
at her I swear I knew then that she was beautiful."*

Dagoberto Gilb spent sixteen years making his living as a construction worker, twelve of those as a journeyman high-rise carpenter with the United Brotherhood of Carpenters. He is the author of The Magic of Blood *(University of New Mexico Press), which won the 1994 PEN/Hemingway Award and was a PEN/Faulkner finalist. He is also the author of* The Last Known Residence of Mickey Acuña *(Grove Press). He has been the recipient of a Guggenheim Fellowship and a Whiting Writers' Award. Recent work has appeared in* The New Yorker, The Threepenny Review, DoubleTake, *and twice in* The Best American Essays. *His new book,* Woodcuts of Women, *will be published in the fall of 2000 (Grove). He is currently on the faculty of Southwest Texas State University in San Marcos, Texas.*

Mi Mommy

I was holding her hand at a train depot. I can still feel my arm in the air, limp and soft with trust. It must have been Union Station, Los Angeles, and I don't know where we were going or why. I was thrilled. I was small, probably just walking, and looking up at her I swear I knew then that she was beautiful. She was wearing a hat, one of those brimless hats that women wore in the fifties that matched the rest of the outfit. Almost all my other early images of her are from the department stores we would go to together—she's trying clothes on, everybody paying so much attention to her, or standing at a cosmetic counter, my mommy and the women around talking so fast and unashamed, giggling, the silver and gold and glass tubes, the jars and sprays, the smallest brushes, the colored powders. In the train depot on that trip to I don't know where or why, the depot was the black-and-white of a dream, and the indoors had the faraway look of the outdoors, its expanse as dusty as a memory. There was a rose in the hat, I'm sure. It wasn't a real red rose, though, but a decorative one, with something lacy white around it.

I saw her, mi mommy, on her knees crawling toward an altar. I was scared. What was wrong? Why was she doing this? It was big, this church, but all I saw was her. I wanted to cry. Maybe I did cry. I'm still scared when I remember. I didn't look around, I squinted and closed my eyes too, seeing only Mommy crawling, stained-glass light, an echo of quiet that hurt my ears. Was I crying?

I think it was La Ciénaga. It was a Spanish name, and the other stores where she modeled—downtown or on Wilshire Boulevard, department stores like the Broadway or Robinson's—didn't have Spanish names. The store did not seem very large. Just elegant. Racks of women's clothes with beads and jewels, collars and sleeves, strings and straps and bows, low in the front, low in the back. I went into the dressing room where all the models were changing from one thing into another for the show that day. I watched them for so long, breathed the cool mist of perfume as they hurried through the step-throughs and pull-offs of dress and undress—the zippers and snaps, the gritty static or smooth wisp of on and off. Skin that was legs and arms, and round hips that cut into small waists, bras, even a breast, and panties that showed that darkened mystery hair. The piccolo of women's voices. I was such a good boy, they said. I was so cute, they told me. I would be such a handsome man, and they touched me. I remember the warmth of their touch, not in the region of a man, but all over, as in a favorite blanket, my fingers scissored onto its nylon end seam to go to sleep, my thumb in my mouth, sucking. Even then I knew it was woman, that attraction and allure, that I loved, my mommy and her friends, her best friend, the woman from Puerto Rico who she could whisper to in Spanish. I was lucky, and I felt safe because my mommy liked me there. But it was this day I remember, because on the other side of the dressing room door, across the main floor, there was an old man in a uniform tinting a display window that faced the street. There were mannequins behind him and he let me go through a half door to sit between him and them. He brushed on the tint, and I looked out at the people and cars passing by on the other side of the window. It was so much fun to be in there, the glass becoming a yellow-brown, that biting, tart odor. I would run from him back to the dressing room, from one scent to the other, back and forth, the fumes subliminal and intoxicating as I ran from the old man with the paint brush and can in the room no one got to sit in to the beautiful women in their underwear.

She loved to go to Hollywood Park, and went to the last race because admission was free. I loved to go too and not just because of the horses, the earth shuddering under me as they left the gate and rode through the finish line. I liked to collect the bet stubs like baseball cards, the losers thrown down, a trail of litter that began in the parking lot until it carpeted the grandstands. I collected fives and tens, win, place, or show. Then I got into the twenty- and fifty-dollar bets. It was hardest to find the ones to win. Wandering the track for me was like walking on a beach looking for unbroken shells. Sometimes we would go down to the general admission area, at the track level, and sometimes we would walk right over to the nicer area, where there were chairs and tables and drinks, and a number of times we'd be invited to sit in the private, glass-enclosed clubhouse. A man would offer to buy us drinks, and I would get a Roy Rogers, grenadine and coke. She gave me the green olives on toothpicks from her drink to eat. The man who bought the drinks for us might say something at a distance first, and then approach. Mostly she just told a waiter, or the man himself, thank you so much, so polite, generously happy about the drinks from the man, but that would be it, and there we'd be, her and me at the races. I was her date. I was her man. Those men, in their suits and their blazers, snugged or loosened ties, stinking in their colognes, snapping bills off silver money clips, they were obvious, stupid, easy even for me to figure out. She might light a cigarette. There were times she smoked and times she didn't. She didn't smoke, though, for the taste. It was a look she wanted. I'd complain that I couldn't find betting stubs. She'd tell me to look around where we were sitting, so I'd go search the top of the starched tableclothes, in the ashtrays, hunting the big losers. One time I found four hundred-dollar tickets to win, creased the long ways.

She was seeing this one man. Years later I would learn that she'd been seeing him for some time, even before she and my father had divorced, which was soon after I was born. His voice was loud by design, like a horn is loud. She would ask me, Do you like him? He took us to baseball games. The Tigers and Angels and Yankees, the Dodgers and Giants and Pirates. He let me hang around after the games and get autographs. He would take us to some games early so we could watch batting practice. The year Roger Maris hit sixty-one home runs I caught one of his BP homers. He was a big man, a fireman, and sometimes we'd visit him at his station. I was too scared to slide down the pole. It was too fat, too thick. I played handball alone in the white room beside the red trucks. He wasn't a bad man, but I didn't like him very much. I couldn't explain why, except that he was so loud when he talked, and even though he would buy me ice cream anytime I wanted it, he was no fun. And so I would answer her. No, I would say.

We were in the kitchen. I was sitting in one of those heavy metal chairs with glossy vinyl covering—we had two of them—and Mommy got mad at me. I was used to this. She had a job now that she was older, in a dental office, and things like this happened because she was tired when she came home. But this time he was there. They were always going out, and I was left home alone with our knobless television and a TV dinner, sometimes two because I was getting taller, flexing muscles I could see in my arms. He'd only come inside our house once in a while, and this time she must have told me to go away, to get out of the kitchen. In that loud voice he told me to do what she said. I sat there. Then he was louder, really yelling. I sat there. And so he grabbed me and I held onto the metal rails under the chair and he picked it up along with me. I'm not leaving! I told him. You don't tell me! I told him. He was furious and my mom was yelling now, too, and she told him to leave me alone and he stopped, dropping the chair and me in it, and then I stood up and I went into the bedroom and I was crying, waiting for her to come. She hit me sometimes, and when she got there that's what I was expecting. Instead she held me and she was smiling. She was proud of me. She said, You're such a man already. And she kissed me over my tears.

∾ ∾ ∾

At school the kids said things. I knew it. I was bigger and more athletic and angry all the time and it wasn't like they were going to say anything much to my face. My mom was a Mexican and my mom was divorced and one time a girl told me her mom didn't like mine and didn't like me, either. I didn't hang out with too many kids. At school I played only with the boys who played sports. There was this one boy—he had his own bedroom and shelves built all around with toys everywhere, every toy, all the best toys, and every ball and glove. He had a basketball, and a hoop on the garage. I would want to play, and we did, but he was soft, blubbery, and I'd shoot alone for as long as his mom would let me. His mom was always smoking and drinking coffee in a stained white mug and talking on the phone and one time I came over and she took me into their clean bathroom and got a washcloth and washed my neck and behind my ears, scrubbed so hard it hurt. She was supposed to be a friend of my mom's, but I knew she wasn't, not really, because the couple of times my mom came by for me only my mom talked.

Sometimes my mom would take me to the Food Giant and buy me a chili dog with thinly grated cheese on the top that would melt in a minute. When she went out—which was a lot—she left me some money and I'd ride a bike down to the Thrifty's and buy a half-gallon square of chocolate ice cream. I don't remember what she thought I should eat. She didn't cook, except on my birthday when she would make chile verde that would stew for so long that the meat was so soft we could eat it for days. She would buy tamales from a bakery on Whittier Boulevard. Some weekends she would make me scrambled eggs with green chiles that she took out of a can. In the mornings, before she went to work and I went to school, when we went to

a coffee shop for breakfast, she'd give me her hash-brown potatoes. Even then, at that hour, men would look at her. Even then,
sometimes, men would come up to our table, squat so that they
could talk to her. Introduce themselves. I was starting junior
high, I had touched a girl, looked at nudie magazines, and I
knew what these men wanted. Such a good-looking boy I was,
they would tell her. When they guessed my age they would miss
by years, and then the talk would be about her beauty—how
could such a young woman have a son this age? She was too
polite to them, and one time I remember this man's eyes, looking at my mom. I wanted us to be alone. I didn't want her to be
polite. I was so mad at her. I was so mad then that I think I never
got over it.

   She'd stopped modeling, and when she and her Puerto Rican
friend got together they talked about the other models getting
fat butts and saggy *chiches*, girdles and falsies. Her Puerto Rican
friend was marrying a man who owned the biggest sailboat ever
and they were going around the world in it. He'd already done it
before. He was so rich he didn't have to work at some job. My
mom had to have a job. It made her tired. But it wasn't just that,
it wasn't only that she was tired from her job. She was going out
on more dates so she was always busy, either working or out. She
talked wistfully about Pancho Gonzalez, the tennis star. Another
of her close friends was supposed to be his cousin. This was a
woman who talked too fast, too much, and she drank and she
laughed wrong. My mom and her both bleached their hair
blond, or platinum, but this friend's was ugly and cheap-looking.
She was a *fea*, short and plump and pimply, but she thought she
was as pretty as my mom. She was bad news, trouble, I knew,
because by then I was smarter and wiser than my mom seemed to
be. This cousin did not help my mom win Pancho Gonzalez, but

they got drunk a lot together. My mom's other friend, the Puerto Rican woman, stopped coming around much. Maybe she was sailing on the Pacific Ocean, maybe not yet, but she was married, and she was rich, and we weren't.

Though the modeling jobs weren't talked about anymore, weren't around, the pretty clothes were. Bills came in the mail daily. I would answer the phone and a bill collector would ask for her and I would say she wasn't home even if she was. She was working for a dentist who was a Mormon, and she was dating him, and two old biddies started coming to our door and coming in and lecturing my mom and I listened to them with her, for her. I answered their questions because she didn't know the answers. She wanted to become a Mormon,.she didn't care how. We went to his house for Thanksgiving, the first Thanksgiving dinner I had ever been to. The dentist's mother had a bun of white and gray hair and a frilly apron just like one of those grandmothers on TV shows. We had to sit at a long dinner table, longer than any one I'd seen on television, crowded with people. It was a feast of full bowls and platters that were passed around and I ate so much turkey and mashed potatoes that it made me sick the rest of my life, but I didn't think it was because I overate. It was because they didn't like her. Well, I didn't like these people from the start. She and I could only talk to each other, and because we stayed so close to each other, they looked at us like we were being secretive, talking in Spanish. After dinner we took a walk around his neighborhood—it was green with overgrown trees and grass and there weren't always sidewalks, and the idea was that he'd get to know me a little—when my mom said something was wrong, that she was bleeding. She assured me it wasn't that kind of bleeding, teased me for not understanding immediately, but he didn't laugh. He didn't like this, didn't want to have to find an open store, and couldn't believe she couldn't have known something like this, wouldn't be prepared. She sloughed that off, wanting to be cheerful. She wanted to make him happy. But he didn't laugh. I don't know what happened after that. This was the man who I'd been lying to new junior high friends about. Before I met him, she had told me that she was going to marry him. He was a dentist, she'd told me. My dad, I'd tell these guys, snooty, was a dentist. I wanted us to be richer than them. After that day I don't remember ever hearing her talk about him again, and I never asked.

Two or three times my mom took me to an old lady's house. It was an old house, with old things, and it took so much time to have polite manners and eat boring food. The woman, she told me, thought I was a bright boy and liked it when I visited her and, she said, I may be getting an inheritance from her. The woman was nice, and I didn't think anything bad about her, yet this didn't sound right to me. By now my mom didn't always seem too trustworthy to me. But I didn't know what else to do, so I went to the funeral parlor with her to pay last respects. There were no other people, and still I felt as though we were being watched like thieves. The casket was open, though I didn't look close. It was like a church, with wooden pews, and crosses, and Jesuses, though no Virgins. My mom's knees went onto the padded kneelboard, and as they did she made a loud *pedo*. I don't think I'd ever heard that from her before. She looked at me and I looked at her and we both tried to hold back. The more we did the worse it hurt, and the stronger the desire to laugh. She kept kneeling there, her hands folded and her head down like she was polite and praying, but really she was giggling and she'd look over at me and we both started laughing too hard. There was no inheritance for either of us.

~ ~ ~

One night, I was watching TV when a man who my mom worked for, who I think she'd gone out with, came to the door screaming about her. She was out on a date, I didn't know a where or a who or a when. He was wailing about money, what had she done with his money. He was drunk and howling and cussing. I knew about drunk because sometimes there were bottles in the house, glasses broken sometimes, laughter. I knew who this man at the door was because he'd shot someone. Mom had told me about him before, and I'd heard her tell her friends. He kept beating on the door, and it finally blew open right in front of me just as a neighbor cop I'd called from down the street came running up. A week later she married a man raised somewhere near Lancaster. I'd never heard of him, I'd never met him before. He was the cousin of a woman she'd worked with. He had the stupidest grin, as stupid as his hick name. What I liked about him was that he asked me if there was one thing he could do for me. For whatever reason I said I wanted him to take me to see Washington, D.C., and he grinned that dumb grin and said he would. I actually believed him. He and my mom went to Arizona for a week for their honeymoon, and after that we moved into the place where he lived. He wore a different, clean, green uniform every day for his job and most of the other time, too. There were deer heads and birds and fish on the walls. Maple furniture, a family table with a bunch of matching chairs around it. He had a son who was a taxidermist and he was proud of him. My mom's new husband was an electrician and a couple of times I worked for him and that's when I heard him tell his working friends he just felt so lucky to be married to such a pretty Mexican gal. Weeks later she was chosen when she went on the TV show *Let's Make a Deal!* When Monty

Hall asked her her name, she told him her new name without a flinch. But she didn't win anything big, twenty or forty bucks, and she didn't get to pick a door.

It couldn't have been too long after that she asked me to go to lunch with her. We hadn't been able to go out together, the two of us, in a long time because of her work, and then her dates, and now because she was so busy with a new husband. They were beginning to have arguments, quiet or out loud, about bills and money, and they each raced to get the mail first. The lunch was with the loud man she'd dated before. He took us to a restaurant. I don't remember the food or whether I had a good or bad time or much of anything about it now, only that when he pulled into the driveway of the apartment building where we lived, where my mom's husband lived, she jumped out of the car and rushed to the front door, and I was stuck in the backseat and this old boyfriend of hers leaned back to talk to me. He told me he loved my mom and he was sorry and he wished something or other, I don't know. It was a speech, I guess, and it seemed as if he might cry or he already was crying, but I told him I had to go, and I got out of his car. Maybe this was why I didn't like him. Big as he was, he was too loud and yet he would cry. It could've been a coupe Thunderbird, and I didn't even enjoy that. I knew things weren't good between my mom and her husband, that she wasn't happy, and I didn't judge her—I figured out that she'd been sneaking out for these lunches before I went with her—but I stopped being around my mom and her husband as much as possible. I never liked the deer meat or the maple furniture or the Hank Snow music and I ate with my new neighborhood friends, stayed as late as I could with them, lots of times overnight. For a while after my mom and her husband separated, we lived in an apartment complex in the south of town and she would just lie on the couch, half-awake, half-asleep, depressed. We didn't talk too much. I had a job, and even though I was getting into fights in high school, and she was getting the vice principal's calls about suspensions and swats and the rest, she didn't really care, and I didn't think it was such a big deal, either.

She married the loud fireman I hadn't liked but who was a nice man and who was almost ten years younger than she was, though nobody ever thought so, who loved her after all this time, and we moved. He bought her a brand-new house and everything that went in it, and it was as if we were rich, though I didn't feel as though anything was mine. It was all theirs. His and hers. He wasn't around very much. He worked hard at two jobs—he drove a Brink's truck, too—and she had all the money she'd ever dreamed of because he gave her his paychecks as if she were a financial wizard. When we were alone, or when she was joking in front of the women who would visit, her old friends and so many new friends—she was the one who made all the friends because she left her door open and everybody loved her—she would say that he could be boring and dull, say that if he wasn't gone most of the time, if she didn't keep him working two jobs. . . . Then she'd laugh, and everyone laughed with her. She always had food, and always a drink. There were jugs of wine, and beer, and other liquors. There was a new blender, the best. He loved to drink with her, too. He loved everything she did, everything she bought, anything she bought, and she bought everything, and he loved her so much. She was the best thing that he could ever imagine happening to him, his life was full of sunlight and colors he'd never seen. If I wasn't around— and I wasn't much, going back to my old friends in my old high school, going to a new job to have my own money, partying myself now, too, playing with drugs and liquor and girlfriends—I was happy that she wasn't worried anymore. Since she didn't have to do anything but please him, she pleased him. He didn't like "spicy" food, so she learned to cook potatoes and roasts. She babied him when he got home from a job, made him feel like he ran the world. They drank together. They talked to each other and had fun when they drank. When she was around him, she became like him. When he thought he should be serious, he droned philosophically about black people and illegal aliens. My mom was an illegal alien, born out of wedlock in Mexico D.F. and baptized at the Basílica honoring the Virgen de Guadalupe. She often tried to stop him when he went off on a long editorial, but it wasn't always worth it to her, and I began to see that she wasn't only my mom anymore, she was his wife.

My mother was becoming a person I wouldn't want to know, and sometimes in anger, lots of anger at me, especially when I didn't go along with everything she had become, married again, when I was reminding her of the past that she didn't want to remember, she'd get mad. One time she got mad at me when I told a neighbor her husband wasn't my real father. I didn't know I wasn't supposed to say otherwise. I was sorry I embarrassed her. I didn't even care about my real father much, only saw him a couple of days a year, but the only times my mother's husbands were "fathers" were when others made that assumption. They were just men to me, part of her life, not mine. Another time, after a year of living in this new house, with this new husband, whatever I'd said or done got her so angry she told me she didn't know where I'd come from. She meant it, too, looking at me like I was an utter stranger, a lousy tenant.

I graduated high school. I moved out. I got a job as a stock boy. I started junior college.

❧ ❧ ❧

On a Tuesday morning, just before dawn, I jerked myself out of a dream. It was so strong I turned on a light and I wrote it down. In the dream, a voice was talking to me, asking me if I wanted to talk to her. Her being my mom. Why wouldn't I? Because we never did anymore, hadn't really talked in decades. When we did, there was nothing but strains and mutual disapprovals, and for several consecutive years there was nothing at all. I'd moved far away, to El Paso. The voice, not my mom's, was asking me questions from my mom, and I'd started responding to the dream, to the voice, and straight to my mom. It was in the form of an interview, her questions and my answers. I answered the voice, Yes, I always loved her. I loved my mommy so much. She had to know that I didn't care about whatever was bad that had come between us, that I would remember only how much I loved her. I was always so proud of her. I said I thought she was the best mommy, the most beautiful woman. I loved her so much. I said I understood everything she'd gone through. Of course I didn't think only about the past, our troubles. Of course I forgave her, and I told her I wanted her to forgive me too. And then I was overcome by a sob that wasn't in my dream but in my physical body and my mouth and my eyes.

Two days later, her husband called me. He was calm and positive. My mom, he said, had been taken to the hospital on Tuesday. She was found unconscious. There was a problem with her liver. She was in intensive care, but he was convinced she'd be fine, she'd be home soon. He just thought I should know. I thought this sounded much more serious and so I called the hospital and got a nurse there and asked bluntly. She said I was right, it usually was only a matter of time, it could be at any moment, though it could also take days or even a few weeks. I asked about the liver, whether it was the usual reason a liver goes. She asked, Well, was she always the life of the party? I got a plane ticket. I remembered a last visit, a year earlier, finding an empty vodka bottle—plastic, the cheapest brand you could buy—in the corner of the bedroom I was sleeping in, where she kept a mountain of purses and shoes and wallets and just about anything else. I found another, most of it gone, behind a closet door that she left open. I rented a car and went to the hospital. She was bloated, her hair a tussle, this woman who never missed a hairdresser appointment, an unappealing white gown tied around her. Tubes needled into her hand and arm, a clear mask was over her mouth and nose. When she saw me her eyes opened. She had no voice, she could not talk. I talked. Years had passed, she knew little about my life. She knew that I did construction work, thought it was all I did, ever, didn't know anything about the other life I led, the one as a writer. I never told her. I was afraid that she would only be his wife, not my mom, and she wouldn't care in the appropriate way. Or that she would be too relieved, and that all those other years I'd been struggling, when she didn't seem to care, when she disapproved of me, even thought I deserved whatever misery that befell me, would be forgotten. I didn't want to give that up so easily. These were the reasons I had told her nothing. But I knew my mom would be proud. I knew she would be so happy for me. I told her that not only was I a writer, but that I had a book published, another one just out. I had won prizes. I had been going to New York City and Washington, D.C. I'd gone there more than once, and I never paid. Her eyes smiled so big. I knew she would like this the most. She always wanted to travel the world. Can you believe they were even giving me money? I asked her. She *was* proud of me, and she was as surprised as I was about it. And then I told her why I really knew I had to come. I told her about the dream I'd had two nights before, on the first night she'd spent in the hospital. My mom's eyes stopped moving. I said I talked to you, you were talking to me, we were talking. She nodded, her whole weakened body squirmed while she was nodding! I knew it, and yet I wouldn't believe this story if I'd heard it. It was such a *telenovela* deathbed scene, mother and son, both weeping about a psychic conversation routing hundreds of miles through the smog and traffic and over the mountains and across three deserts, from one dream to another, so that we wouldn't miss telling each other for the last time before she died. She was as stunned as me, as happy as me. You know? She kept nodding, looking at me, crying. Oh Mom, I said.

Junot Díaz's mother, Virtudes
Photographed in Santo Domingo, 1964

"I can't even honestly say that it was her words alone that
got me going again but when I look back on it now this assessment—
that she was the one who helped me jump-start my life
again—doesn't seem that wild or wrong."

෴෴෴෴෴෴෴෴෴෴෴ JUNOT DÍAZ

Junot Díaz is the author of Drown *(Riverhead Books), which is published in Spanish as* Negocios *(Vintage Español). His fiction has appeared in* Story, The New Yorker, African Voices, The XXII Pushcart Prize *(1998) and* The Best American Short Stories *1996, 1997, and 1999. He has been the recipient of the Eugene McDermott Award and a Guggenheim Fellowship. He currently teaches creative writing at Syracuse University and is working on his first novel. He lives in New York City.*

How (In a Time of Trouble) I Discovered My Mom and Learned to Live

I.

I spent my senior year in high school pretty much fucking everything up. I stayed home when I should have been in class; I didn't do any work; I fought with my teachers; I fought with my peers; I had a wise fucking mouth. By the time October rolled

around I'd gotten demoted out of the honors program—first nigger in, first nigger out—and put into the "regular" classes where
I did nothing except stare at the walls and read Stephen King
books. *It* was the last book I read in high school, which should
tell you something about my state of mind. (*We all float down
here.*) I was nineteen, having stayed back a year because of my
Spanish, and was adolescent skinny and adolescent ugly. No
pulchritude of face, no pulchritude of clothes. And man, our
poverty. Ever since my pops had bailed my family had become
eighties-Reagonomics broke. Anybody who's lived through that
period knows what I'm talking. Those were tough years to be a
poor person of color, especially tough if you were an immigrant.
You know it was bad because white folks weren't *even* trying to
be us. Things were pretty desperate. There were mad mornings I
cut school just because I couldn't bear the thought of wearing
the same shit I'd put on three days before. So on those days,
instead of heading to the bus stop (ever since my brother had
checked into the hospital me and my boys had been forced to
take the bus because none of us had the loot to keep his
Monarch on the road) I walked out to the landfill and stayed in
the woods as long as I could stand it. On rainy days I trooped
down to the Sayreville library and poked around the stacks. I
remember being especially enamored with Doris Lessing's *Canopus in Argos* series, the design and heft of those hardcovers. I'd
found them one day while looking for something else to read
besides King. I remember taking them down and wondering how
the hell could this be science fiction. I was too intimidated to
read the books themselves but I liked to keep them near me
when I was in the library and reading something else. I think
this was the only openly hopeful gesture I made in those days.
You have to understand: I was in an emotionally "difficult"

period. Blame it on adolescence, on poverty, on young person of color self-hate, on my father's departure, on whatever—I was the gloomiest kid around and there were times I couldn't imagine living past the age of twenty. Those books at my elbow were some sort of promise of a tomorrow when I might actually feel smart enough and confident enough to read the whole series. A tomorrow when I might actually feel *good* about myself. No doubt this was a ghetto nerd's tomorrow but it was the only one I had.

I was also angry. Almost all the time, so angry that after most of my days I fell easily into dark exhausted sleep. I was especially angry at my father for leaving and at my older brother for losing fifty pounds and only then being diagnosed with leukemia. Rafa was up in Newark, in Beth Israel, on the top floor of the hospital so that when you pushed your face against his window you could see the burned-out blocks, the scarred-over reminders of '67; and New York's skyline, a million brick middle fingers pointed at the world.

2.

My moms had her own problems. Because of my brother and because of the economy and because the locals weren't trying to hire non–English speakers, she couldn't work full-time. So we were Section Eight, los cupones, AFDC all the way. She was still grieving over my pops. The nigger had pretty much shipwrecked her—abandoning her in a state where you needed a car to survive, where she didn't have any family nearby, in a neighborhood cut off from any economic tides whatsoever. And while I might not be the best judge of these matters, I believe this was one of the darkest periods in my moms' life. Years later, when I interviewed her for my book, she still claimed the Dark Age was 1965. The year of the Revolution. When I mentioned 198–, she got quiet. Yes, she said. Those were bad times, too.

My moms was a tiny woman—later, when I started weight-lifting for real I'd be able to curl her—and she was as light-skinned as you could be without being able to pass for white. When my brother was still around we used to call her the Queen of the Bata because it seemed she never got out of hers. She'd come to the United States because of us, but I don't think the move had ever given her much happiness. She was a silent woman, never spoke of herself or her heart and for most of my life the only "facts" I knew about her were that she was my mother and that she didn't play around. (Once she'd mentioned that when she'd been little she'd won a jacks competition but the next time we kids brought it up she pretended like we'd heard wrong, said to us, I never won anything in my life.) My pops I knew a lot about but of my mother I knew nothing. All of my friends talked about their pops, we compared them like we compared everything about ourselves, but unless our moms cooked well or hit us they didn't get no public play at all. I felt like Claire in *Abeng*, but unlike her I accepted my moms' silences as a given, assumed that's all she had to give.

That last year of high school I watched my moms a lot, though. I didn't have anything else to do. I was tired of my boys, they were tired of me. Me and her spent a lot of time tranqueado in our apartment. Mornings she always got up at the same time and I listened to her moving around up above me. She washed up, made her coffee and then tuned in to Radio WADO, which in those days was our primary bridge to the rest of the Latino world. On the days she went to visit my brother she'd leave me an egg sandwich on the stove and then one of her friends or the taxi that the Medicaid paid for would pick her up and I'd slip out of bed and watch her from behind the curtains. She always waved at the driver; she might have been quiet and worn-out but my moms was a friendly woman and the niggers who knew her, liked her. She visited my brother three or four days a week and always on weekends. But before she left she would knock on my basement door and say Levántate, muchacho. Every damn morning the same thing. Levántate.

But somedays I'd oversleep and when I woke up she'd be sitting on the edge of my bed, right next to me. Her presence never surprised me. As if, even in my sleep, I could feel her near me and know not to be alarmed. Our basement was extremely dark and she'd be nothing more than some breathing and the dark cut of her hair but I'd know it was her. Señora, I'd say and she'd put her hand on my face.

She, I see now, was watching me too.

We fought a lot. As you can imagine. She'd have her rages over my father and our situation and I'd have mine over everything. Doors slammed, nights spent out with friends, TVs raised high. We were a couple of fuckups living in the ruins of our lives. There was a lot of shame too, more than I can discuss here comfortably.

In April I learned that I hadn't been accepted to any of the colleges I'd applied to, not even Rutgers Livingston, which in those days was us niggers' safety. Even though I'd fucked up my grades—I mean, I failed whole classes that year—I'd honestly thought I'd get in *somewhere*. I was, after all, smarter than my boys who *had* gotten into school. What arrogance. When those letters came, I don't think I talked to anybody for a week. Just locked myself in my basement for six straight days, and when finally my boys came for me one night, forced me to take a ride with them to the Shore just so that they could cheer me up and tell me that the world wasn't over, it had been so long since I'd been outside that I remember that the streetlights hurt my eyes.

When I told Mami about the rejections I said to her, Well, it looks like I'm fucked. I went on to blame her *and* my father *and* my brother *and* the school, while she watched me and said nothing. Finally she went, You should have worked harder, which only sent me into a bigger louder fit. Neighbors banging on their walls, my mother retreating to her room, another night with my boys, drinking in the backseat of a car.

Graduation Day I refused to attend the ceremonies down at the Garden State Arts Center—which was where the rich-ass school that I was being bused into held their shit—stayed in bed despite my mother's upset. In the end she went without me. Caught a ride with somebody else and when they called my name, mispronouncing it as always, my boys told me she nodded once and put both hands on her purse. I still remember what a beautiful day it was—the sun was everywhere, driving deep and hard into the bricks. I took a walk down to the Sayreville library and stayed late. When I got back Mami was in her room, no longer dressed up, watching her novelas. She heard me come in, I'm sure, and I heard her TV. I went downstairs and waited for my boys to call.

She didn't talk to me, really talk to me, for a long time after that.

Such was our lives.

3.

I don't know how much time passed. Enough, I can assure you. I worked delivering pool tables by day and at night I took drives with the boys that remained. We headed out all over New

Jersey and had the usual Parkway-Turnpike adventures. Every now and then I sat with my newly returned brother, tried not to stare at his ravaged body. The rest of the time I was in my basement, trying out the new loneliness of my post–high school life.

Sometimes when I got off the M15 coming back from my job my moms would be getting off the bus coming from hers. She shaded her eyes with her hands and said, Hijo, and I tipped my head and said, Señora. We walked home in silence, me between her and the road. Sometimes I'd get off the bus and she'd already be halfway up that long curve that was Ernston Road and I'd follow her at a distance. We both had crazy jobs but hers was worse, cleaning houses for professors and middle-class people, and when she got home she always cooked dinner while I sat in front of the TV and watched *Doctor Who*. Now that I didn't have to hide out I didn't go to the Sayreville library no more. (The next time I'd see *Canopus in Argos* I'd be in college and the tan spines of those books staring from the stacks would hit me like a right cross to the chest.) Whatever it was that was around my heart in those days—an armature of anthracite, a crust of gyprock— didn't feel like it was going to crack anytime soon. I decided this would be my life for the next couple years and was miserable because of it.

4.

I can't tell you how many times she tried to talk to me. It was hard for her, you know, to have one of those pat sit-down mother-to-son chats, the kind the TV was always insisting were possible; sit-down chats weren't a part of the family repertoire; we just weren't brought up that way. We were Dominicans and Dominicans, at least the ones I knew, don't really talk to their kids. Mami tried. She'd wait for me to be watching TV, usually at night, when she thought I'd be my calmest, and then she'd sit down at my side and I could see it coming a mile away because she'd have this serious look on her face. Look, she'd say, you have to struggle if you want—

I usually didn't let her get any further than that. I'd either put my hand up and tell her to leave it or I'd go downstairs without a word. It was easy to hurt her; after all, she was my mother. For some reason it felt good to leave her midsentence on the couch, to have her follow me onto the stairs and say things like, I didn't come to this country so you could quit. What about college? I used to shout at her, It's not like you even went to school. My moms certainly didn't need that kind of shit from me. She was barely keeping her own self above water. Money was mad tight and even with government help cancer medicine wasn't cheap. It was like we couldn't win: everytime my brother got released from the hospital he caught a flu or an infection and had to be taken right back. Lots of nights I could hear her walking around upstairs when she thought I was asleep, could hear her moving from the bedroom to the kitchen to the porch and that never stopped her from dressing for work in the morning or from knocking on my door and saying, Levántate, muchacho.

5.

In the end it was just some words that did it.

Can't tell you nothing about that day except that I was coming back from another one of my useless nights out and my mother was sitting on the couch watching the main TV; the shit was so busted-up that we couldn't turn it off, had to lower the volume when we wanted to sleep. It was this huge horrible neversleep cyclops in the center of the room. My moms was still as a bone and her hair was dark and wet from the shower and as I headed down to the basement she said, with some bitterness, You know, I cried less when I lost my first son.

I heard her say it, but I didn't answer back. I sort of shrugged and headed downstairs, pretended like I didn't know what the hell she was talking about. The TV stayed on for another hour and then she headed back into her room for some more TV and finally sleep.

That night I lay in bed and stared at my walls. *You know, I cried less when I lost my first son.* Like I said, I didn't know nothing about my mother. That I'd had another brother who had died was a huge shock even to hard cold me. That she'd never mentioned him in all these years was something else altogether. Said a lot about the kind of relationship niggers like me have with their moms. I always used to claim that I loved my moms, told everybody this, but how in the world can you truly love somebody you don't even know?

This is a short piece so it's not like I can fill in all shades or hit you off with crosshatchings galore but I'll tell you one thing: That night was the first time in my life that I had to deal with the possibility that my moms was a person and not just somebody who washed my underwear and cooked my meals. She had a world inside of her, I realized. A world. It was like suddenly finding yourself in a depth of water. It was an astonishment.

My mother had surprised me similarly once before, back in Santo Domingo. I didn't remember that earlier incident right then, but I do remember it now. This was back in our Villa Juana days. I remember we were on a bus going somewhere and my mother pointing at another neighborhood and saying, This is where my old novio used to live. She didn't say nothing else and even then I was taken aback by her statement. I'd always thought my mother had known my father her whole life.

The next day we had breakfast together. Avena and some toast. Radio WADO was on and so was the volume on the TV. Come out here and look at the birds, my mother said. She was sitting on the porch. I followed her outside and stared at the sparrows, those ubiquitous flying woodchips. When I was grown I'd hear about it—the first pregnancy, the Invasion, the bomb falling—but right then we didn't speak about my dead brother and we wouldn't for many, many years.

6.

I can't say our relationship changed much after that night. Our world still sucked and it continued to suck for a long time afterwards. We didn't suddenly become best friends. I can't even honestly say that it was her words alone that got me going again but when I look back on it now this assessment—that she was the one who helped me jump-start my life again—doesn't seem that wild or wrong. Because sometime in those next couple of months I started making small moves, nothing too radical, little changes that slowly began adding up. The first big obvious one was that I stopped lurking around in the basement so much. I stopped hating my boys for their hard work and their college acceptances and brought myself back into the fold. I bought a car and started taking night classes at Kean College. (Certainly, you say, words alone can't have this power. Somewhere in my heart I must have been ready for this change and Mami only facilitated the emergence of what was already there . . .) Eventually I was able to transfer to Rutgers–New Brunswick, a dream of mine. But by then a lot of the other shit had cleared up as well. I was still angry, still an emotional mess, but I'd learned to hide it somewhat, not to let it paralyze me as much as I used to. Sure, my pops never came back and the old brother I'd known before the chemo never did either, but after a couple of years I'd begin to talk to my mother seriously and a couple of years later, we'd even become friends.

Gioconda Belli's mother on vacation in Portugal
in the early 1960s

*"It took me a long time to separate from her enough
to see her longing for a life she never had."*

Gioconda Belli was born and raised in Nicaragua. She is the author of three novels and five books of poetry. Her work has been translated into eleven languages. Two of her works, The Inhabited Woman *(Warner Books), a novel, and* From Eve's Rib *(Curbstone Press), a collection of poetry, are available in English. She is currently at work on a memoir to be published by Knopf.*

Just a Woman

My mother was at a baseball game when her labor pains began. "It took you so long to come out," she tells me. "Two long days." "You were so ugly," my father says. "You were so hairy. You had hair on your cheeks, on your ears, you looked like a little monkey. People who came to see you commented that you had nice hands. They were being polite, trying to find something nice to say about you. You did have beautiful hands. Long fingers. You had the hands of a pianist, of an artist."

"Your father paced the room carrying you in his arms to soothe you when you cried. He would talk to you," my mother adds. "He would say, 'My poor baby. You are so ugly, you poor

169

thing.' Your brother had been such a beautiful baby. Blond, blue
eyes. It was such a contrast, and yet you were the girl." "But you
shed all that hair from your face and your ears pretty soon," my
father says, "and you were so smart, so good. Such a good soul."

Parents. It's through them that we first see ourselves. I have
heard the story of my birth as a monkey countless times. I loved
to hear them tell it. And they assumed they could go on telling
it because I was no longer ugly, because it was my own personal
Ugly Duckling Turned Swan story. From a very early age, however, I remember sensing that they worried about me a lot, as
though I were something fragile, an object of concern, as though
they knew that I was destined to get into trouble. And they
knew it from the beginning.

At six months, the nanny dropped me, so they say, and I had
meningitis. "Your father wouldn't sleep, wouldn't stop crying
until you were finally stable and had no more fever."

Then, when I was two, I split my lip playing bullfight with
my older brother. I was the bull, and when he lifted the towel he
was using as a cape, I went straight through and hit my mouth
against a table.

"Your father was so afraid you'd be disfigured. We took you to
the best doctors. They immobilized your hands for a month so
that you couldn't touch your face."

At three, I swallowed a coin. It obstructed my pyloric valve.
No food could be digested in my stomach. My father wouldn't
hear of an operation. There was a physician in Philadelphia who
had earned a reputation for extracting foreign objects from the
body without surgery. My mother and I flew to the United
States. The procedure was successful.

I had an appendectomy at nine, and at fourteen I fell in love
with the wrong boy.

⌒ ⌒ ⌒

Jimmy is an aspiring biologist with a passion for reptiles. He is my older brother's schoolmate. At the country club he's the only boy I know who can swim the crawl in a straight line across the Olympic-sized swimming pool, not once, but several times. He has an athletic body and wears a very brief blue bikini. He dives from the highest board in perfect form, without bending his legs. He's tanned and, because he spends so much time in the sun, strands of his blond hair are bleached almost white. My brother and Jimmy are fast friends. They share a passion for water. They go to the beach together.

Jimmy comes to our house often. Sometimes he brings one of his pet snakes along, a big boa carried around his neck. My mother hates snakes with a passion. She can't stand the sight of them, can't stand the fact that Jimmy dares to show up at our house with that reptile crawling all over him. She finds him suspicious and strange. "Who in his right mind would choose such a hobby? There must be something wrong with him. He takes such liberties, getting a glass of milk from the refrigerator as though he were in his own home." I cringe when I hear my father and my mother talk about him. I like him. I don't want him to be banished from our house.

Of all of my brother's friends, Jimmy is the only one who's noticed me. He thinks I'm cute, intelligent. He talks to me. He's already shown me how to distinguish a snake that's poisonous from one that isn't. One day there's an item in my brother's school newspaper that Jimmy is head over heels for me. A friend mentions it during the morning break at school. She's all excited. I don't believe her until she borrows a newspaper from someone so she can show me. See, see, I told you. I see it with my own eyes. I've made it into the boys' school newspaper. I exist at last. I'm not a monkey anymore. My eyes are not so small, my nose not so big, my lips not so wide. Somebody has seen through my shyness, my quiet demeanor. Somebody has seen the woman budding behind the ugly school uniform, behind the girl who spends weekends at home, reading book after book.

The next time I see Jimmy, I blush but I don't run away. I wait for him to say something and he does. He apologizes for the boys making jokes about it—but what can he do? He says it's true. He likes me a lot. He thinks I'm wonderful, very special.

By this time, I'm completely in love with him. I'm a romantic heroine and he's my beau. No matter that my mother hates him, that my father despises him, that I'm told it's completely out of the question, that, at fourteen, I'm not allowed to have a boyfriend, least of all Jimmy, Mowgli, the boy from the jungle, snake charmer, dangerous Jimmy.

Jimmy and I have not even held hands, but one afternoon he proposes that we run away and get married. He says it's the only way. We can leave the house right then and drive to Tipitapa.

Tipitapa was the town of choice for desperate teenagers. One of my classmates just got married there. It's about three in the afternoon on a Saturday. My mother is out shopping. My father always takes Saturday afternoons off to have beers with his friends. We are alone in the house. We're sitting on metal rocking chairs on a stone terrace outside the living room, sipping Coca-Colas. Jimmy is very calm. He seems so grown up. His voice is low, soft, very seductive. I rock back and forth on my chair. I'm so tempted to say yes, but I'm terrified of my parents' reaction. My mother has already warned me of my responsibilities as a woman, bearer of life. Generations of men and women will spring from my womb. She has made me see that my descendants will curse me for centuries if I don't choose the right mate.

I'm too young to choose. I can't make a sound judgment at fourteen. However much I disagree with my parents about Jimmy, I know they are right about that. The clock is ticking. "We don't have much time," he says. But I know that time is the only thing I have plenty of. I don't have to hurt him, to refuse him. If I simply wait long enough, my mother will come home and I won't be able to leave with him—which is exactly what happens.

I don't know if my mother saw right through me, but soon after that I was the one who was banished.

'm on my way to boarding school in Spain. A great privilege, a great honor. Of all my brothers and sisters, I'm the first to go to New York and then to Europe. No mention of Jimmy. My parents are so convincing in their arguments—it's for my own good, a tremendous opportunity—that I don't make the obvious connection. So I go along enthusiastically, feeling incredibly lucky and blessed. Europe is a magic word for me, a good-luck charm. If you get a European education, you'll make something worthwhile of your life. Most of my friends were happy just to go to the United States and learn English, but my parents wanted something else for me, something loftier: real refinement, real culture. I feel very proud when I break the news to my classmates, who are all very impressed. They dream of going to finishing school in Switzerland, but most of them will have to make do with student exchange programs, a summer spent living with an American family, not so much because of financial constraints, but because their parents can't bear to send them so far away for so long. I bask in the glory granted to me by my mother's snobbishness. Both my parents have conveyed to me the importance of persevering, not giving in to sorrow or sentimentality. To rise above the norm I have to be willing to make some sacrifices, to be strong.

Jimmy sends me desperate love letters. I'm sad about our romance, but he can't compete with Europe or with my desire to grow up and set sail into the unknown with my parents' blessings. I'm not ready to defy my parents. I think too highly of them. I'm a good soul, a good and grateful daughter.

"After you've seen New York, nothing will ever leave you dumbstruck again," says my mother. That's why we're going there first. My mother metamorphoses into a soaring creature when she travels. In Nicaragua she sleeps late, hates to exert herself, and languishes for long hours in air-conditioned rooms, reading plays and dreaming of doing theater, her passion. As soon as the plane has taken off, however, and she feels safe at cruising altitude, she puts away her crystal rosary beads, takes out her Fielding guide, and reads avidly to prepare herself for the task of dealing with the unknown wonders that await us. She doesn't want to feel out of place or act like a tourist. She wants to be worldly, to know how much to tip, where to go, how to proceed.

I can barely keep up with her. As soon as we arrive in Manhattan she wants to walk, to go to museums, to go to Central Park, to go shopping. She's a small, slim, distinguished-looking woman who loves pearl necklaces and Hermès scarves. She's been a blond for most of my life, although her natural hair, which I have only seen in old photographs, is a light, reddish chestnut. She has an angular face with high cheekbones and a long classical nose. Her hands are long and slender.

Her English is impeccable. My mother was one of the few women who finished high school in a time when girls married in their freshmen or sophomore year. She had gone to an exclusive girls' school in Philadelphia, run by the same order of nuns that ran the school I attended in Nicaragua and the one I would attend in Spain. Cory Aquino and Grace Kelly had been my mother's classmates. She boasted that she had been invited to Grace Kelly's wedding. I don't know if she really was, but the Nicaraguan newspapers reported it as a fact.

At that time, I professed a humble and deep admiration for my mother. It took me a long time to separate from her enough to see her longing for a life she never had. She was a Madame Bovary of sorts, but cultured, altruistic. She fancied herself a patron of the arts, and also explored her own artistic potential. She painted and made mosaics, organized a theater group, acted, directed, adapted plays. She wanted to transcend the limited boundaries of Managua society, my father's simple preoccupations, the constraints of domesticity. She fought with all her might to be a woman ahead of her time, but at a certain point she gave up the fight and perished, sickened by a life that no longer held the possibility of dreams.

When I was fourteen, though, and we were on our way to Europe, I thought my mother had everything she ever wanted. She made me think she did. There were no cracks in her armor yet, no signs of weakness. She was a tower of strength, indefatigable, eager to see and learn for herself, and to compel me to take full advantage of all that life offered.

She had no patience for my adolescent whining or my uninformed opinions. She dragged me through New York, Amsterdam, Rome, Paris, Madrid, to see everything she had dreamed of seeing: the Metropolitan Museum, the Rembrandts, the Vatican, the Louvre, the Jeu de Paume. I followed her obediently, hating her at times, swearing to myself that I would never visit another museum as long as I lived, unable to take in everything. She wanted me to absorb it all at once, as though this were my first and last opportunity.

I was not then and have not since become a good tourist. I like to take my time, to linger, to stand in a room without knowing its history, to close my eyes and let the atmosphere penetrate me, listening for the echoes of ancient sounds that I sense will manifest themselves to me if I just take the time to be there lovingly, appreciatively—not like the tourists who seem to be making check marks on a list of places and things someone told them they should see.

My mother had a list of her own, but it was, nevertheless, a to-do list. It didn't allow for much lingering. Besides, she had purchased vouchers for sightseeing tours in every city, so we went around like anxious cattle following guides who raced through historical places and museums, as if they were on an obstacle course. In the evenings, my mother took me to the opera, to the ballet, to musicals. One night in Paris she dressed me in black and made me up to look older so that I could be admitted to the Folies Bergère. She considered the burlesque show an art form that should be part of my education. She was a truly avant-garde woman

Climbing up from the Atocha train station in Madrid through a narrow and winding street, we arrive at the boarding school. It is an imposing, austere, gray building. The heavy doors of the convent close behind us with a hollow sound that echoes in the pit of my stomach. The walls of the entrance hall are covered with antique white, blue, and yellow tiles. We are shown into a visiting room with a dark wooden floor. The place is so silent we talk in whispers. A nun comes to greet us dressed in the purple robes and ivory veil worn by the order of the nuns of the Assumption of the Virgin Mary. She shows us around the school, the dorm. "She will sleep here." The nun turns to my mother with a smile. The cubicle has two low walls and a curtain that opens onto the common hallway. Inside, there's a narrow bed, a washbasin, a commode, and a window overlooking the small garden in the back. My heart drops inside my chest. I already feel like a modern Jane Eyre.

A few days later, my mother leaves Madrid. We say good-bye in the visiting room. A nun was with us the whole time to help me in the separation. I have a sinking feeling in my stomach. I can't believe my mother is going to leave me there and fly back to Nicaragua the next day. The whole Atlantic Ocean will be between us. How can she be so calm? Not a tear in her eyes. I swallow my own tears. My mother thinks people who cry are overly sentimental and without self-control. It's not in good taste to cry. I watch her disappear behind the massive wooden doors. I hear their hollow echo closing me into that gray, cold, foreign world.

Shortly before she died, my mother told me she had known I would get into trouble ever since I developed the habit of looking at the world upside down. "You were eight or nine years old," she said. "You were always lying backwards on the furniture, on the beds, with your head hanging off the edge, imagining what it would be like if people walked on ceilings and had their mouths on their foreheads. You were always wondering what it would be like if things were reversed. You wanted the world to be different. You had a contrary spirit."

I had been visiting my parents in Nicaragua. I walked into their bedroom and slumped into my father's wide, blue reading chair facing my mother. She sat before her dressing table. It was her favorite place to sit, a director's canvas chair placed directly in front of the open door to the patio. "I'll tell you what I remember of my childhood, and then you tell me what your memories of it are," I said to her. She was puzzled. She must have thought it was a strange request coming from a thirty-seven-year-old woman. "Please. It's important to me," I insisted. "All right," she said, crossing her legs, folding her hands on her lap, as if she had been asked to take the witness stand.

The solitary mango tree in the background looked dark and listless in the yellow dusky light of the Managua sunset. My mother shot me a defiant look. Like the tree, she also seemed lonely, a small, frail, ailing woman in her sixties, still managing to look elegant, well groomed, her blond hair perfectly coifed, a diamond solitaire on the middle finger of her manicured hands. Her only concession to afternoon leisure was the beige leather house slippers she wore.

"When I began to look at the world upside down, I had just discovered that I would be me forever," I said. "It dawned on me one day, on the way home from school, that I couldn't change who I was; that I could not enter into anybody else's head or body. I was to be Gioconda Belli for good. The notion made me reel. I felt trapped, alone, powerless. It took me some time to see the advantages, to start enjoying being who I was, the secrecy of my own mind like a cave where I could hide and where no one else had access. No one except you," I said. "You could open me up. You knew the magic words. At first, it was a comforting feeling, but as time went by, I sensed you as a threat. I sensed you had a power that could do me or undo me." It was hard to tell my mother about the struggle to discover what it was inside of me that belonged to her; what commands, what ancient designs she had passed on that I had to outgrow in order to allow my own self to take over. "It was from you that I got what I feel is most mine," I said, "the things that define me the best. It was you who gave me my sense of strength, of power. But then there were the contradictions. I had to find my own way among them. I had to know where I stood. Me, not you."

She leaned back on the chair. She seemed softer now; no longer on guard. Just a woman. If only I could see her like that, I thought, release her from the power she unknowingly, unwillingly, commands. If only my daughters could do the same with me.

Frida Agosín carrying baby Marjorie at the
National Zoo in Washington

*"Some day you would tell us about a childhood that lay suspended
in somber whispers and frightful secrets."*

Marjorie Agosín was born in Valparaíso, Chile. She is the author of Always from Somewhere Else: A Memoir of My Chilean Jewish Father; A Cross and a Star: Memoirs of a Jewish Girl in Chile, *and* The Alphabet in My Hands: A Writing Life, *as well as several volumes of poetry and stories. Her nonfiction work includes* Tapestries of Hope, Threads of Love: The Arpillera Movement in Chile 1974– 1994 *and a collection of essays,* Ashes of Revolt. *She has edited and coedited numerous anthologies, including* The House of Memory: Stories by Jewish Women Writers of Latin America; Landscapes of a New Land: Short Stories by Latin American Women Writers, *and* What Is Secret: Stories by Chilean Women. *A winner of the Letras de Oro and the Latino Literature Prize, she chairs the Spanish department at Wellesley College.*

Frida, Friduca, Mami

Before you appear, a delicate fragrance infiltrates the corridors of the house where dark and secret things dwell. Mami. You are always there with your scents that change with the rhythm of the seasons. In the spring, orange blossoms rub against your childlike bare knees. You tell us stories. "Girls," you whisper, "we are disobedient *sultanas* dancing through the palaces of Córdoba and Granada."

Your games ranged over the centuries, through the secret thresholds of so many spoken and unspoken stories. In the summer you smelled like the almonds that fell on the moss surrounding the house or like the nectarines and cherries always in blossom. You rested in the winter, and decorated the house with violets, the flowers of old women. But even when you, too, were old, you thought you were different, as if you feared making an alliance with the laments of time.

Who were you, Friduca? Were you that angry woman who threw the enormous Santiago telephone guide at father because he came home late? Or that other woman who, frantic with happiness, undressed and drank Portuguese *vinho verde* while she sang boleros in German from the balconies?

So much of your story is wrapped in small, mysterious, and smoke-filled postcards. When we asked you to tell us tales that were not about dragons and magical coaches, you said that some day in a bed full of feather pillows, you would tell us true stories that were more frightening than ghosts. Some day you would tell us about a childhood that lay suspended in somber whispers and frightful secrets. Many years would pass before we knew what stories persecuted you in your frequent nights, when you wandered through the house in search of restless ghosts or of girls like you who wore yellow six-pointed stars on their coats.

In the summer you would bring us to the Pacific Ocean. Like your mother you were afraid of rickets. You believed in the sun and in the constellations that you often pointed out to us and named out loud. And now, under this foreign Northern Hemisphere sky, I remember the three Las Pascualas, the three Marías, and the Southern Cross.

In the beach house surrounded by cacti and lizards, we felt that we belonged to you, while in the winter, you withdrew from our laughter, or approached us restlessly, dazed, as if your body were calling you to other places. But the summer before our exile, your life and ours were not to be forgotten. We became your allies and confidants. We drank beer and you told us that the golden foam came from the gods. You also let us grow our hair long and wear white pants. That summer while we clung to you, we also discovered who you were.

One night when the wind and the sea echoed unspeakable sounds, we asked you to tell us your own story, not one made up of fairies and dragons. You muttered, grew silent and then said that you would tell it to us in episodes, like Sheherazade who had tried to save her own life by telling stories. So, you began:

"My father was an old Viennese gentleman. He loved Goethe's poetry, the German language, and pretty cabaret dancers. That is why he came to Chile, to the Pacific coast of South America, to escape from many lovers. When he saw the young brides, the white washerwomen, descending from the illuminated hills, that the mules climbed carrying pitchers of water, he said this would be his country. He swore to love the Spanish language and Valparaíso Harbor with its run-down houses and midnight owls that adapted their song to the music of the sea."

You smiled sadly and continued.

"We belong to a persecuted and not necessarily chosen people. The history of our people has been distinguished by the most unnamable horrors of war. My grandmother Helena wore high-heeled shoes and loved strawberries. She lived happily in Vienna until she could no longer go to her beloved garden and had to embroider a Star of David on her coat. The restrictions against Jews began slowly, but eventually they lost their citizenship. One restless evening, thanks to divine Providence, my grandmother and her children made the long journey from Vienna to the port of Hamburg where they boarded a steamship that would rescue them from certain death. The boat headed for Valparaíso where they would be met by my father whom you know and love.

"I will tell you," Mami said, "about the afternoon when we went to Valparaíso Harbor to wait for Helena." She choked from emotion and grew faint, as if this were part of a story she had carried deep within herself. Covered by goose bumps, she continued. "The whole family gathered at the harbor that day. It was Sunday and the street vendors sold balloons and sweets as though the city were in a festive mood to receive them. My father, wearing his Viennese gentleman's hat, paced. He was so anxious to see them that he decided to call a tugboat to bring us to the ship. At that time I was thirteen years old and my brother Jaime was eleven. We boarded the tugboat and the wind howled as it tousled our memories and brought us closer to someone who had been furrowed by grief, our grandmother, whose name I had seen only on faded postcards.

"And suddenly there was her veiled hat fluttering in the breeze. She wore an elegant velvet dress with a sequined dragon pinned to the neckline. She had few possessions, and carried the eiderdown quilt that she had shared with my grandfather, Isidoro Halpern, in a worn-out straw basket. I kissed her on the cheek and she prayed in German while kissing me on the forehead. In that instant, the wind stopped conjuring up secrets, and a passion for her arose in me that has never left me. My grandmother and I became inseparable. For years we shared the same room, the same laughter, and the German and Spanish words we taught each other. We also shared the silences, the memories, and the conversations with her dead sisters.

"In the evenings Grandmother Helena would gaze out the window that faced the tall palm tree in the garden and make strange shrieking sounds that seemed to come from her womb. It was very hard for me to reconcile myself with those perverted nights in which she would kiss the keys that she always carried tied to her apron strings. When she became senile, she would put the keys in her son's pockets and accuse him of all types of wrongdoing.

"My dear children," Mami would say, "I have lived among the dead and among memories that tell only of the dead. I have lived among scorched gold teeth and false addresses. Nothing is known about the lives of my aunts. I wonder if they died from fright when they arrived at the camps of fear or if they perished in the gas chambers. Your whole life, you have asked me questions that I cannot answer. My childhood stories were not inhabited by angels with immense gossamer wings, and I never dreamed that some day my loved ones would return. I also have asked myself, Who am I? Where is my soul? Whom do I resemble in the family photograph? And why have I never returned to see my aunts? Like a pilgrim, I have tried to assemble the puzzle of my own history, to learn about those knives that cut into the darkness, and why my grandmother cried when she lit the Sabbath candles. I can't tell you anything more because my tongue was also stilled and because uncertainty was a mad truth that constantly threatened us."

That summer on the Pacific Coast was memorable and unique. Mami didn't enter those wrenching silences, but continued talking to us. Shut up in her room in broad daylight, she told us strange things—like how her cousins from Prague had arrived at her house in southern Chile, and how her father would greet malnourished women refugees at the train station with large baskets full of flowers. I associate my language with her memory. Perplexed, we listened to her, although many years would pass and many more stories would be heard before we came to understand her. My mother was sometimes like a little girl, sometimes an eccentric woman who didn't like talking with the neighbors, but would nevertheless engage in long conversations with strangers whom she would never see again.

In that summer of 1970 we discovered many things. I fell in love with a boy who told me stories about Che Guevara that were either true or false. My sister learned about the Berlin Wall and my brother about a camp on the outskirts of Prague where child prisoners painted butterflies. My mother decided to devote herself to the joys of living. She spent hours contemplating the moon and the stars scattered across the heavens. She ate strawberries at midnight and happiness arose from sweet smells carried by the gentle breeze. One day she took us on a walk to the sea. She said that all great roads led to the sea. She told us to fill our pockets with shells, imaginary crystals, and starfish, and to make wigs of floating algae because through this delightful game we would acquire the peace of the entire universe.

Mami taught us about the astonishment that is linked to the unexpected and about the presence of certain warning signs that should be heeded, in the secret rhythms of lizards in love or in the iridescent face of sunflowers. That afternoon she told us about the times when she would accompany her grandmother to the Red Cross offices to wait for news of the war. She told us how at the end of the Second World War, she and her classmates had marched in a huge parade in Santiago, carrying baskets filled with red carnations, how the sidewalks of the city had been transformed into floral necklaces and red carpets in memory of the dead. Perhaps she thought about how the Nazis had interrupted the lives of her aunts forever.

It happened one day in the middle of the afternoon, when they came home from piano class. Eva, her youngest aunt, was taken to the Gestapo Office, never to return again. Somehow, through these stories, I grew to understand my mother's silences, her early-morning reticence and her obsession with knowing we'd all arrived safely at home, where she would shut the doors and breathe deeply at last. I sensed that life was a miracle, that we were forever being saved from an imminent catastrophe, that life had its dangers. Mami told us this whenever she entered into that place of profound exhaustion dominated by her solitude.

The winter passed, the violets blossomed, and autumn arrived, covering the ground with a blanket of leaves that we stepped on as we came out of school. The earth was like a screeching violin playing an arpeggio for our mischievous feet. One day we changed schools, no longer attending the British Institute where we had constantly been made to salute and curtsy, and where once, as we left school, our classmates had surrounded us in a hallucinatory circle, shouting and spitting: "Jewish dogs, Jewish dogs." I remembered then what Mami had said, that life was full of unexpected dangers. I also believed that catastrophes were always just around the corner, waiting to happen.

Another summer arrived and we returned to the house at the seashore where Mami ate juicy watermelons. One day at the beach of the agate stones she said, "These stones remind me of the crystal street lamps on Castro Street." Lying on the sand wearing the copper-colored sweater that matched her hair, she told us about her father's precarious situation after he brought his mother, brother, and other refugees to Chile. He had fallen deeply into debt financing visas for their safety. But he had maintained his dignity, never let on how bad things really were. He simply looked for another future in the crystal lamp business.

"My father bought antique glass in the elegant neighbor-hoods of the Chilean aristocracy. He arrived home daily with iridescent violet, mauve, and yellow crystals after an exhausting day as a street vendor. And all of us, including Grandmother Helena, climbed to an upstairs attic that almost touched the sky, where we threaded those crystals onto delicate wires. We didn't sell any lamps, but in the afternoons we opened the window to let the rays of sunlight enter the crystal room and listened to the teardrops of light chiming in the wind. Amid all our poverty, this spectacle of the floating crystal conjured a generous beauty." Mami began gathering the agate stones again, and as she opened and closed her hands, she counseled us to always appreciate the unexpected wonders and gratuitous goodness of nature. That was the last story she ever told us.

Then one day in the early seventies, the soldiers came to Chile. They wouldn't let my brother grow his hair long like the Beatles and they wouldn't let me wear pants. In our neighbor-hood, afternoon book burnings became a common sight. The police were obliged to burn books that were considered danger-ous. My mother remembered her grandmother's escape from Vienna on Kristallnacht, the destruction of her beautiful library. Where have the words gone?

Mami became more silent and hostile. She stopped talking to us and devoted herself to organizing the first "garage sale" in Chile. She said that refugees didn't need things. That is why she sold the tablecloths, the figurines, the dolls, and the fine china. She kept only a few silver trays brought from Morocco by a friend, a samovar bought from some Gypsies, some postcards from Vienna, and the blue-covered notebook in which she and Grandmother Helena kept the wildflowers they gathered on their secret walks. Our departure from Chile was imminent. It was then that I realized why Mami had taken so long to tell us her story. Perhaps she had been afraid that everything she told us would come true again.

Although I was too young to understand how things were, I understood that asking questions was forbidden, and little by little I began to penetrate a universe of fear and inertia. I realized that I should start saying good-bye to certain things, to beloved trees and streams. I decided to make copies of the keys to my house and desk. These would be the sacred objects of my memory as they had been for my great-grandmother Helena who had died in her late nineties with the keys to her house tied to her diminishing neck. Mother lost the radiance in her violet eyes and her voice became serious. She no longer walked around the house barefoot. At night, I heard her praying in German with the voice of an angry, dispossessed woman.

And one day we left. I don't remember precisely the hour of our departure or the month, as if my memory had been severed. We were all disoriented and speechless. I only remember that certain people came to say good-bye: our closest friends and my beloved history teacher, Martita Alvarado, who arrived wearing a red coat and carrying a white notebook which she gave to me so that I would write about the genesis of my new history. That timeless night we blended with the immensity of the heavy silence around us. Very few relatives came to bid us farewell. Perhaps they felt it was absolutely necessary to conceal our departure. Frida, you had already returned to take charge as you had done on the nights of grief and sorrow before we left. You kept saying that every journey is the beginning of a better life. Perhaps this is how Grandmother Helena felt when she set out on her uncertain voyage to the Southern Hemisphere. We, too, were traveling to an unfamiliar country. No river would caress our feet as the rivers of the south had done, and never again would the scent of jasmine and violets emanating from our mami tell us we were home.

The Andean range darkened as we departed. The sky was a basket of shadows. I felt that I was repeating the story of my Viennese great-grandmother and my Russian great-grandfather. Perhaps you were right, Mami; perhaps for a while it was better to learn stories of fairies and dragons than the true story of our fate, of the history of Jews like us, without a homeland. We had been driven into exile by politics, not racism, but like our ancestors we had become wanderers, travelers.

We came to North America. There the people laughed less and Mami, you seemed to laugh more. We lived in an empty house with plastic chairs. It was very hard to fill it because we didn't have any guests. Instead of singing boleros in German, you cheered up by dancing the *cueca* and the tango and by passionately remembering all that you had left behind. When other children made fun of my height you would say that they were poor little things because they didn't know that I was magical, a relative of Thumbelina. And when they laughed at our accent, you said that they were less fortunate than we were because they spoke only one language.

In the house in Georgia you planted *boldo*, bay leaf, cilantro, and violets, and we smelled your familiar fragrance once more. We learned to love this new land that provided us with shelter and human warmth. Miraculously, we survived once again, and learned to name other stars. Our happiness was hidden, less exuberant, but we survived.

Now in the U.S.A., I tell my children stories. They think I make all of them up, even though some are true. Sometimes I say: "Children come close, I want you to listen to me. Be my confidants. Come, bring the pillows from Casablanca, elixir from Córdoba and the fans from Madrid. . . . Once upon a time there was a mother who lived in a country with five thousand volcanoes and many penguins . . . a beautiful and luminous country with blizzards and archipelago islands. That country had a wise ruler who died in a palace set ablaze by a powerful, conceited dictator. Like many other citizens, we left and crossed the mountain range in search of safety. Life is full of wonders, mysterious cliffs and miracles. . . ."

In those moments, I know that you were close to me, Mami, and I knew why you had to hide your stories. You are like a bridge to all those secrets. As I call you, the room begins to fill with the scent of violets and jasmine, and you tell me that it is time to leave the dead behind, to bid them farewell, and to sit down to eat at the table of the living.

The years have passed and you have remained near us in the earth that we seed, in the birds that visit us at daybreak. Above all, we have preserved your memories and your voice in this both strange and familiar room, in the foliage of the trees. Your stories have marked the path for all the possible returns, and here in the yard behind the house we see you hanging out the clothes to dry. We see you pruning the rosebushes, saying: this is where my responsibilities end; now it is time for *you* to tell *me* a story.

Translated from the Spanish by
Celeste Kostopulos-Cooperman